Paul Nesbitt-Larking. 6.50

Teachers, Professionalism and Class:
A Study of Organized Teachers

Jennifer Ozga
and
Martin Lawn

The Falmer Press
A Member of the Taylor & Francis Group

This book is dedicated to our parents.

First published 1981 by Falmer Press Limited (a member of the Taylor & Francis Group) 4 John Street, London WC1N 2ET.

ISBN 0 905273 20 6

Jacket design by Leonard Williams

Printed and bound by Taylor & Francis (Printers) Ltd, Basingstoke, Hampshire.

Contents

Introduction

This book is an attempt to generate discussion and research on organized teacher activity, an area of study within education which remains relatively neglected, particularly in terms of reputable studies of union activity on a day-to-day local basis. We believe that part of the reason for lack of discussion in this area is that the characterization of teachers as professionals, opposed to union activities, has become the orthodox view, which dominates the literature to the extent that teacher union activity is polarised into two opposing areas, the 'professional' and the 'union'. In the first section of the book, which reviews much of this literature, we want to make several separate, but related, criticisms of this approach:

firstly, in adopting 'professionalism' as a defining concept for teacher behaviour, authors in this field have made little serious attempt to explore the meanings of that term to different groups at different historical periods. This criticism applies equally to authors who uphold 'professionalism' as model behaviour and condemn militancy, and those who condemn teachers for attempting to become professionals, as this separates them ideologically from the working class. Neither group of authors is prepared to investigate the way in which professionalism could both operate as a strategy for control of teachers manipulated by the State, while also being used by teachers to protect themselves against dilution. Secondly, we feel that many authors, be they historians, sociologists or pressure group theorists, have, consciously or unconsciously, adopted a favourable attitude towards professionalism, which leads them to neglect aspects of teacher union behaviour which they see as irrelevant. The dominant assumption is that teachers have consistently struggled to achieve professional status and have identified themselves as professionals rather than union members. From this assumption others follow: for example, teacher unions are not politically aligned and operate not through sanctions but by responsible consultation and cooperation, while recent outbreaks of militant action represent the irresponsible behaviour of the young rank and file and reflect the bitterness of teachers who have failed to achieve full professional status. These discussions of teacher unionism also stress a conflict between professionalism and unionism which is perceived as fundamental, hence, teacher union behaviour is consistent when following the 'consultative' pattern of the 1940s and 50s, but deviant when embracing strike action, as in 1910–20, and in the 1960s and 70s. There is no discussion of the possibility that 'professional' behaviour may simply represent an orientation of union action rather than an alternative to such action.

Finally, while these points raise criticisms of the way in which professionalism has been used as an explanatory concept, we feel that an approach which took into account its different meanings, at different times for different groups, could lead to progress in understanding organized teacher behaviour beyond the sterile dichotomy of professionalism versus unionism which dominates the literature at the moment. In conjunction with such an approach it is necessary to assign a role of considerable importance to the State in developing the education system in response to the changing needs and structure of capitalism. Within such a context the most fruitful way of understanding the behaviour of organized teachers is in terms of employer-employee conflict, which leads to attempts by teachers to resist State interference. The State may disguise its essential relationship with the teachers by manipulating those aspects of the professional ideology which stress teacher autonomy, while teachers may resist State intervention by making use of a defensive argument based on possession of professional expertise. The fact that both the State and the teachers make use of the same term does not mean that they are essentially in harmony, the conflict is disguised, and often the State uses its buffer sub-government, the LEA, to further conceal the true nature of the relationship.

While we place the State at the centre of events, we do not see it as incorporating the teachers within it, as State personnel, or members of the ideological State apparatus, or members of the new middle class oppressing the working class from whom they are supposedly separated ideologically. Though we think it fundamental to an understanding of organized teachers that an analysis of teachers' class position should be developed, and we review attempts to do this in our second Chapter, we are critical of much of the material produced to date within a broadly marxist framework which, with its emphasis on a division between mental and manual labour and its assumption of the existence of a new middle class, characterizes teachers as oppressors of the working class and puppets of the ideological State apparatus. This literature draws on assumptions about professional status and union behaviour which are surprisingly similar to those developed in the conventional historical, sociological and pressure group studies. In addition, both groups of writers neglect detailed investigation and analysis of teachers' work and working conditions and their struggles for education against the State in both the past and the present. In the second half of the book we attempt an initial development of an account of teacher unionism based on giving prominence to teacher resistance. In the historical section, we draw attention to some of the alliances between organised teachers and the working class and the Labour Party, and to examples of teacher militancy. We discuss the State's response to the growth of teacher militancy in the period 1910–1920, through the fostering of professional, responsible behaviour in return for a measure of 'autonomy'.

In furtherance of our theme of recognizing the fundamentally antagonistic relations between employer and employee, we investigate the parallel development of white collar unionism to illustrate the complexity of problems faced by these workers and we develop the points of similarity between teachers and white collar workers as an introduction to our final section which discusses the concept of proletarianisation and its application to teachers. We argue that – as the State's use of professionalism as a controlling strategy declines in the context of economic crisis and the scapegoating of teachers for failure to retrieve an economy, itself in a period of decline, and as teachers' objective conditions of work are radically altered – the behaviour of organized teachers comes closer to that of other organized workers and conflict between the State and the teachers is no longer so effectively concealed.

Obviously, contradictions and ambiguities among teachers, in terms of their own class identification and their interpretation of their relationship with the State, remain. We are not setting out, in these two short sections, to 'prove' an alternative historical explanation or to 'prove' that teachers, like other white collar workers, are proletarianized. We merely wish to suggest that these are alternative approaches which might generate rather more discussion than the assumption that teachers are either caught between professional behaviour and union strategies or constitute the ideological oppressors of the working class. In addition, a great deal more investigative empirical work needs to be done to establish exactly how organized teachers themselves use the concept of 'professionalism' and to see how teachers' perceptions of their relationship with the State change in a period of teacher redundancy and redeployment unparalleled since the 1920s. We believe that such investigation would support our steps towards a reinterpretation of events, in the light of a perspective which takes the State's antagonistic relations with its employees as its central focus and which sees that characterization of the essential relationship as constant, though the strategies adopted by both sides may alter the superficial appearance.

One final note; we have limited our discussion to organized teachers and, though some of the authors we review do not make this distinction, most do. Hence, most of the published material available deals with teacher unions and their members and we did not wish, except where it was unavoidable (i.e. the characterization of teachers as members of an ideological State apparatus) to extrapolate from the discussion to include automatically all teachers. We also wish to make the more positive point that it is in teacher unionism that the teachers' own record of confrontation with the State is revealed, while membership of the teacher union itself is a basic step towards a recognition of class interest and combination in defence against the employing class.

Further, though we are advancing a general argument, the material we draw on – as well as being restricted to published sources on teacher unionism – is further restricted by the fact that these sources refer only to teacher unions in England and Wales and not throughout the United Kingdom.

PART ONE

Chapter 1.
Organized Teachers:
A Review of the Literature

This chapter looks at the major published sources relating to teacher union activity from three broad perspectives which we have characterized as:

1. The Historical Approach

2. The Sociology of the Professions

3. Pressure Group Theory

Though some of these studies were published some time ago, they continue to be influential, as can be seen from a glance at journal articles on teacher unionism or at the titles of M.Ed. theses in the area. Despite the different origins of the authors of these studies, we suggest that there is a broad convergence of views between them and that, moreover, the essential interdependence of their views has led to the establishment of an orthodoxy which is only now being questioned, particularly by critical trends within the sociology of the professions and by Marxist, or neo-Marxist, historians. The dichotomy between professionalism and unionism has inhibited examination of teachers' own perceptions of their working conditions and working relationships, and how these have changed and altered over time. Instead, discussion has been focussed on two opposed, ill-defined abstractions: 'professionalism' and 'unionism'. In this review of the literature, we wish to reveal the assumptions on which that discussion was based.

Our argument is that the concept of professionalism is an extraordinarily complex one and its different meanings must be located within a specific historical context. Thus, its use as an ideological weapon aimed at controlling teachers must be appreciated whilst, at the same time, it should be understood as a weapon of self-defence for teachers in their struggle against dilution. Such appreciation of the complexity of professionalism and its multiplicity of meanings is, on the whole, lacking in the studies which we review in this chapter.

The Historical Approach

The major works in this category are by Thompson (1927), Tropp (1957), Roy (1968) and Gosden (1972).[1] These authors each deal with the historical development of teachers' unionism (especially the NUT) in parallel with the growth and development of state provision of education. They provide invaluable secondary source material for any student of organized teachers. However, they make little connection between change and development among organized teachers and developments in society generally and among the organized labour force in particular. These studies either characterize the teachers' unions as 'reactive' bodies, responding to central government initiative, or as a group following an almost predestined path to professional status. As aids to explanation of the growth of unionism such studies are useful but limited and their limitations become more apparent when we attempt to apply their conclusions to more recent organized teacher behaviour.

Tropp's study outlines the gradual development of teaching as an occupation and the range of his study, from 1800–1950s, lends weight to the impression of consistent progress towards professional status – measured by the various education acts, by increasingly stringent regulation of teacher qualifications etc. His overall position is indicated in this quotation:

> It [the profession] was created by the state, and in the nineteenth the state was powerful enough to claim almost complete control over the teacher and to manipulate his status while at the same time disclaiming all responsibility towards him. Slowly, and as the result of prolonged effort, the organized profession has won free and has reached a position of self government and independence.[2]

The driving force behind the 'prolonged effort' is never fully analyzed, nor is the role of the state, in monitoring or controlling or resisting this effort, discussed.

Yet some considerable attention is devoted to ensuring that we fully understand that the 'prolonged effort' was neither class – nor political-party-based. Both Tropp and Roy share an overwhelming concern to establish the non-aligned nature of teacher unionism. Roy, an influential NUT executive member, is anxious to stress this point:

> This investigation has revealed that the NUT is free from the influence of party political pressure groups to a remarkable extent. It has successfully resisted attempts at communist infiltration, and the communists today have neither control nor a powerful voice in the higher councils of the union; among the rank and file, there is hostility to communism as such. The rejection of moves to affiliate either to the TUC or the Labour Party represented the clear majority, though the TUC affliation is again under active consideration. When it comes to the political questions of the day, there is a firm stand against party political involvement, and an attitude of keeping out of party politics at all costs, based partly on a teachers' conception of his job (his professional status) partly on his instinct for self-preservation at a time of encroachment by the major parties on the educational service, and partly on the recognition that the greatest danger to professional

unity comes from alignment with political groups. However much it may be accused of sitting on the fence, it can face a whole complex issue [secondary reorganization] in the knowledge that it is itself an organization free from any party political ideology or party bias, and without worrying about the serious internal problems, which, in other organizations, are caused by party political pressures.[3]

As Beryl Tipton[4] remarks 'leaving aside the subsequent election of a communist president and decision to affiliate to the TUC, this interpretation creates a feeling of dissatisfaction'. Ms. Tipton is concerned about Roy's 'image building' as a member of the executive, and feels that a greater political consciousness among both executive and rank and file members must exist. Tropp shares Roy's 'non-political' position, stating that whenever teacher unions have appeared to deviate from the policy of political non-alignment in the past by alliance with organized labour, this has been for purely strategic reasons and represented no political commitment on the the part of the union concerned (the NUT):

Each alliance has been for a specific purpose as were the alliances of the NUT with working class groups during World War I and during the 1942–44 campaign for education advance.[5]

Tropp, Roy and Gosden all promote the impression of organized teachers acting consistently in a non-political,

5

non-class based movement towards professionalism. It is not surprising, then, that authors looking at organized teacher behaviour in the late 1960s and 70s see strike action and sanction implementation as a new departure.

The difficult question of the class position of teachers is not satisfactorily discussed – Tropp defines teachers as middle class and, thus, non-party political. In the same way, no definition of 'professionalism' is attempted, except in terms of increased control by teachers over their own affairs and decreased control by their employers, yet the similarity of such aims to those of the organized workforce in general is not remarked on.

Donna Thompson[6] shares the general approach of Tropp, Gosden and Roy and, in describing the growth of the NUT, reduces the significance of some events whilst elevating others into a general theory of professional development. From her reading of 'The Schoolmaster' and NUT reports she finds evidence of 'The professional spirit which has always characterized the organization'.[7] Although these sources also demonstrate the incidence of strike activity and alliance with organized labour in the period 1912–20, Thompson interprets the NUT's action in this period as 'resembling' a trade union but distinguished from it by an overriding professionalism and concern for education exhibited by 'the dignified way it has conducted its affairs even when using the strike weapon'.

Thompson at least discusses the NUT's strike action but emphasizes that the union always recognized 'the relationship between the welfare of the general public and their own interests'. However, her overall treatment gives less of an impression of irresistible progress along the professional road. Poor pay, poor promotion prospects, extraneous unpaid duties and no control over qualifications are all characteristics of the teacher's job to which she gives attention. In addition, she characterizes the state's role as one of stringent control, quoting Sir George Kekewich's description of the Board of Education as always 'on the watch to find something which deserved a lecture or chastisement'.[8]

The class origin of the majority of teachers is acknowledged by Thompson who claims that, in consequence of the adverse conditions of work experienced by teachers, 'a class consciousness, though feeble, was beginning to develop'. Yet, in Thompson's conclusion, professional status remained the overriding, and *preferred*, aim to extended union activity. She sees the two as contradictory, the claim for 'professional' status is not seen by her as a likely extension of union activity and she rejects the possibility that it could be pursued in alliance with party politics or the labour movement (though she is unusual in even considering this):

> the past policy of the union has been, and its present policy is, to achieve a self-governing profession, and while this aim might be achieved if the union were more closely allied to labour organizations, yet it would seem that this policy can be pursued best if the union is not pledged to any labour or political group.[9]

A rather different approach to the growth of teacher

unionism can be found in Beatrice Webb's 'New Statesman' supplements on the teaching profession.[10] The NUT
is identified as a trade union, formed in defence against
such state-controlled systems as payment by results and
against the power of local managers. She also focuses
on the social isolation of teachers, caught between the
working class of their origins and the middle class they
are presumed to aspire to. Beatrice Webb examined the
structure of the NUT, and concluded that, like manual
trade unions, it used 'mutual insurance and collective
bargaining, with the ever present alternative of the
strike'.[11] The 'professional' claims of the union, as demonstrated by demands for a register and increased status
are dismissed by Beatrice Webb as 'manifestations of a
professional egoism in the teacher which tends to impair
the social value of his service'.[12] Webb also analysed
what she perceived as a change in the pattern of behaviour
of the NUT.

> The Trade Unions of the workers will more and
> more assume the character of professional associa-
> tions . . . each trade union will find itself, like the
> NUT, more and more concerned with raising the
> standard of competency in its occupation, im-
> proving the professional equipment of its members,
> 'educating their masters' as to the best way of
> carrying on the craft, and endeavouring by every
> means to increase its status in public estimation.[13]

The interesting point she makes about the *general* trend
of trade unions to assume professional characteristics,

thereby indicating a possible convergence of union and professional interests rather than a dichotomy between them, has not been followed up, nor has the similarity of these NUT aims to the traditional aims of craft unionism been adequately discussed. However it appears that Webb, herself, saw such an alteration in NUT behaviour as a deterioration, and disapproved of the shift from direct to indirect action:

> like a trade union (the NUT) is not above bargaining with a local authority, and frequently supports individual teachers who refuse to accept certain terms. Though it has even in one case in the course of half a century organized a successful strike it has steadily subordinated this direct action to the indirect pressure exercised by teachers' representatives in Parliament and on the local authorities, and by perpetual deputations and representations to the Education Department and the Local Education Committees.[14]

The 'indirect pressure' exercised by the NUT in pursuit of its professional aims receives a great deal of attention from writers in this category, as we have indicated earlier: strike action is barely acknowledged and the activities of local associations, over terms and conditions of service and salary negotiations, are of only secondary interest. Press publicity, public meetings, union sponsored MPs, deputations, contacts with the Board and the LEAs 'the friendly conspiracy' are all emphasised (and responsible, consultative, collaborative behaviour comes to characterize the NUT) an approach which lends support to those authors in our Political/Pressure Group category who perceive the union(s) as part of the educational sub-government or a 'Third Estate' in education.

To sum up, despite some discussion of the problems of 'class' and alliances with organized labour in both Thompson and Webb, the dominant paradigm of organized teacher behaviour which emerges from the major histories of teacher unionism is of a gradual progression towards a middle-class, non-aligned, 'professional' group, rejecting traditional union (working class) strategies and adopting professional models of 'indirect' pressure. In putting forward such a case a great deal is taken for granted, and a great deal left unexplored. The class position of teachers, particularly elementary teachers and their 'emerging class consciouness' is not a question that has been subjected to close scrutiny until relatively recently and offers alternative insights on the historical material available to us. So also does the question of the congruence between white collar and craft union strategies and the behaviour characterized as 'professional' by historians of the teacher unions. Within this literature, the concept of 'professional' is never defined, nor is there any serious attempt to make connections between 'professional' ideology and social class position – beyond Tropp's assertion that teachers are middle-class and therefore non-political. The vagueness of these authors towards a definition of 'professional' stems in part from the fact that they make 'common sense' assumptions about its meaning and use. It is obvious from their writing that some attributes – such as responsibility, client-orientation and ethical behaviour – are connected with, and to some extent define, professionalism. These positive attributes are allowed to shape their selection and perception of evidence and lead these authors to underrate seriously the importance of other events and directions within teacher unionism. The same favouable bias towards professionalism as a concept is apparent among sociological studies of the professions, to which we now turn.

Sociology of the Professions

An enormous literature has been produced under this heading, and it would not be appropriate to attempt to review it all here. Our interest lies in demonstrating the changes in approach to the sociology of the professions, from trait theorists like Millerson,[15] Carr-Saunders and Wilson[16] to Johnson's[17] analysis of the professional's role in relation to state capitalism, and Larson's[18] discussion of changes in the nature of professionalism in response to changes in the capitalist state. Obviously, not all of the literature is directly relevant to the discussion of teacher unionism as many of the studies do not concern themselves with organized teachers or even with teachers as an occupational group. However, these studies are important to us because they have done much to reinforce a static and positive concept of professionalism and have disguised its internal contradictions and ambivalences. It is significant that sociologists have found it so difficult to arrive at a definition of 'professional' which is not a reflection of the morally good qualities attributed to the leading professions by members of these professions. Further, additional work done on the basis that such value-laden criteria distinguish the 'true' professionals has supported the dichotomy between professionalism and unionism, and given additional weight to both the historical treatment of teacher unionism outlined above, and the pressure group analyses discussed below. Yet, when most of this work on the sociology of the professions is critically examined, it is found to be of limited value.

A great deal of effort was expended by devotees of the *trait approach* to the analysis of the 'professional'. Briefly, such an approach involved the attempt to isolate the distinguishing characteristics of a profession. Flexner, one of the originators of the 'trait' approach, isolated six criteria for distinguishing professions from other types of occupation. In his view, professional activity was basically *intellectual*, carrying with it great personal responsibility; it was *learned*, not based on routine; it was *practical* rather than purely theoretical or academic; its *technique* could be taught, thus providing the basis for professional education; it was strongly *organized* internally; and it was motivated by *altruism*, professionals viewing themselves as working for some aspect of the general good.[19] The many attempts to evaluate the degree of professionalism, which could be claimed by a given occupation on the basis of this and similar catalogues of attributes, all resemble one another in one way; they give high 'scores' to the traditional professions, such as law and medicine, while certain occupations, like teaching and engineering, do not quite come up to scratch. Most trait analyses are, in effect, a catalogue of those desirable attributes accorded to the medical and legal professions by those professions. This effectively demonstrates the inappropriateness of the attempt to isolate 'professional' as a scientific concept which could be defined by a precise list of characteristics, isolating an abstract and objectively discriminate class of phenomena. The trait approach was closely connected with structural-functionalist sociology in that it assumed the existence of a relatively homogenous group whose members shared identity, values, definitions of role and interest and who were governed by norms and codes of behaviour. Such an approach rules out conflict within the group or between that group and competitors attempting to secure its privileges for themselves.

The *'process' approach* to professionalism, developed by the Chicago School, attempted to break the deadlock by concentrating on definition of the *process* which occupations went through in order to achieve professional status. This, at least, had the merit of recognising deliberate activity on the part of the group involved. Various attempts to arrive at a clear definition of these stages were made but the strategies isolated were almost all those which had been successfully adopted by law and medicine. An interesting consequence of this approach was the spread of the idea of a line of development eventually leading to full professional status – the *'natural history' approach*. By this analysis, some occupations were 'in process' towards professionalism, but were impeded by such undesirable characteristics as high female membership (nursing, teaching) and significant levels of unionisation (teaching, engineering).

One of the few studies to draw on this work and apply

13

it to organized teachers in England is Parry and Parry's[20] article on 'Teachers and professionalism' which argues that:

> The teaching profession have been deeply influenced by a conception of occupational ideology and organization which we shall call professionalism.[21]

Parry and Parry resemble the authors in our historical section in that they, too, are confident that teachers have pursued a consistent strategy for development as an occupational group and that this strategy may be defined as 'professionalism'. They argue their case on the basis of the historical evidence which they present concerning the teachers' Registration Movement. However our interest lies more in the fact that they reject the functionalist approach to professionalism and identify professionalism as *an occupational strategy*.

> Professionalism, in our definition, is a strategy for controlling an occupation in which colleagues, who are in a formal sense equal, set up a system of self government. This involves restriction of entry to the occupation through the control of education, training and the process of qualification. Another aspect is the exercise of formal and informal management of members' conduct in respects which are defined as relevant to the collective interests of the occupation. In addition, there is use of occupational solidarity and closure to

regulate the supply of services to the market and which serves also to provide a basis for the domination of institutions, organizations and other occupations associated with it. Finally, there is the reinforcement of this situation by the acquisition of state support in order to obtain, if possible, a legal monopoly backed by legal sanctions. Where this is not possible, at least the tacit acquiencence of the state is required.[22]

What is unconvincing about this article is firstly, the assumption that teachers embraced a *professional* ideology by attempting to achieve the objectives listed above and, secondly, the selection of one (unsuccessful) movement, the TRM, as the evidence to support this thesis. It would be possible to make a case, using the same definition as that quoted above but as a description of craft/white-collar unionism and to demonstrate the failure of such unionism as an occupational strategy through the failure of the NUT to affiliate to the TUC throughout the same period.

However, the discussion of the state in Parry and Parry's article is of interest as their treatment represents a recognition of state intervention in determining 'professional' status. Indeed, Parry and Parry develop this idea in an illuminating concluding paragraph, where they ascribe to the state a vested interest in manipulating the teachers fruitless pursuit of professional status on a 'divide and rule' principle.

The stark fact now is that the state, having become

the most powerful force in education, has a vested interest in opposing the ideal of the teachers' registration movement, in blocking the establishment of a self-governing teaching profession. It is difficult to conceive of any way in which the basic situation is likely to change, and it remains the underlying reason why the occupational movements of teachers have been organized on the model of unionism.[23]

But why is this 'model' less threatening to the state? Most unions resist dilution and attempt some control over entry and training – this question is not even raised by the Parrys, who conclude that:

Teacher unions in Britain still aspire to professionalism but the overwhelming importance of them is, in itself, an indicator of the failure of teachers to achieve the object of professionalism.[24]

This conclusion neatly demonstrates the extent to which the Parrys have accepted the conventional dichotomy between professionalism and unionism, despite their desire to escape from the difficulty which they perceived in other writing on the professions, which had been 'cast in a manner which had given writting or unwitting support and articulation to the professional ideology'.[25]

To the extent that the Parrys blame teachers' disappointment at the failure to achieve professional status for 'the outburst of militancy which has sometimes characterized union activity in recent years',[26] they also lend support to the professional ideology. But the idea of a positive role assigned to the state in manipulating teachers' pursuit of a professional ideology at least indicates a new avenue of exploration which has been developed by Terry Johnson.

We shall concentrate on Johnson's work on the state and professions contained in his book *Professions and Power*.[27] He has developed his work in the direction of class analysis of the professions, particularly that group which he calls the 'state professions', but we will discuss that work when we come to discuss the whole question of the class position of teachers.

Johnson, in *Professions and Power*, devotes the first part of his book to a crushing critique of functionalist and trait theory approaches to the study of the professions. His critique rests mainly on the fact that such approaches assume a functional value for professional activity across all groups and classes, thereby excluding any treatment of the power dimension, and they do not provide 'any means of analysing real variations in the organization of occupations in culturally and historically distinct societies'.

Johnson goes on to elaborate a theoretical framework for the sociology of the professions which concentrates on identifying and accounting for those institutionalized forms of *control* which, he argues, define professionalism.

> Professionalism, then, becomes redefined as a peculiar type of occupational control rather than an expression of the interent nature of particular occupations. A profession, then, is not an occupa-

17

tion, but a means of controlling an occupation.
Likewise, professionalization is a historically
specific process which some occupations have
undergone at a particular time, rather than a
process which certain occupations may always be
expected to undergo because of their 'essential'
qualities.[28]

Johnson presents a typology of forms of control –
collegiate, patronage, and *mediation.* This last category, and
particularly its most significant exemplification in state
mediation, is of particular interest to us. Johnson argues
that mediation occurs when the state intervenes between
practitioner and client in order to define needs and/or
the manner in which such needs are catered for.

It may do so with a minimum of encroachment
upon an existing system of *professionalism* . . . the
effect of intervention may be to support for a time
at least the existing institutions of *professionalism.*[29]

Is there a connection to be made here between the
Parrys' assessment of the role of the state in exploiting
'professionalism' among teachers on a divide and rule
basis, and Johnson's argument that mediation creates
a category of 'state professionals', whereby various occupations are increasingly incorporated into the organizational framework of government agencies, with all that
implies in terms of financial dependence and commitment
to bureaucratic roles?

Megali Larson's[30] analysis of the rise of professionalism

attempts to disentagle the nature of the 'mediation' between professionals and the state. Like Johnson, she rejects the 'static' notion of professionalism, and argues that the nature of professionalism has changed in relation to the changing nature of capitalism. Thus, the entrepreneurial professions grew and flourished in the liberal or competitive phase of capitalism in response to the needs of the bourgeoisie. They fostered the ideas of altruism and objectivity, so often associated with professionalism, in their drive to win client support and trust in a society increasingly organized on market principles. These qualities may be subscribed to by modern professionals but they are residual qualities; the essential nature of modern professionalism is its dependent relationship on the captitalist state, which has itself emerged as the agent of corporate or monopoly capitalism, which is capitalism in its most developed form. Thus modern 'state' professionals are to be found in state bureaucracies; both professionalism and bureaucracy being, in Weberian terms, highly rational forms of organization. Within the state, professionals play an important role in determining the structure of society in response to the needs of the capitalist mode of production, particularly through the social selection mechanism of education. In addition, the ideology of professionalism, which contains contradictory residual elements from earlier phases in the development of capitalism, acts to deny the importance of class conflict by opening up the possibility of 'professional' status to all classes, and by stressing the accessibility of educational opportunity. Thus professionalism, in its modern form, is highly important to the capitalist state.

Teachers, Professionalism and Class

In its modern form professionalism is compatible, and not in conflict, with the state and state professionals carry out the most important functions of the state as agents of capitalism. In addition the ideology of professionalism serves to deny the existence of class and class conflict. However there are residual elements of the 'old' professionalism within the new modern state professions, and this sets up contradictions and conflicts. State mediation fosters dependence on the state rather than independence and autonomy.

According to Johnson, state mediation also has the effect of encouraging divergent interests within the occupation and inhibiting the growth of a 'complete (organizational) community'. This, Johnson argues, produces practitioners with very different orientations towards their tasks and different degrees of identification with their occupational community. He uses social workers as an example but teachers also seem to fit fairly well into his argument, particularly as he goes on to make several points of particular interest in relation to teachers:

> Under this form of institutionalized control (state mediation) the functions of occupational association in maintaining colleague identification are likely to be less important than are its specifically 'trade union functions' in pressing for improvements in pay and conditions. The functions of bestowing status and identity are sometimes shared with agencies other than the occupational association or are completely taken over by agencies such as the employing bureaucracy . . .

Where the functions of maintaining standards are taken over by state agencies, or are provided for in legislation, the association is transformed into an occupational pressure group, effectively losing its powers to prescribe the manner of practice. The degree to which trade union functions do become dominant will depend on the degree to which the state is involved in determining the manner in which occupational services are to be carried out ...

Where state mediation creates large-scale bureaucratic service agencies, it is likely that practising members of the occupation will no longer be the chief service of technical advance in the field, as in the case under *professionalism*. The practitioner loses initiative in the development of knowledge to full-time research institutions ...

One of the major ideological orientations accompanying state mediation is a stress on social service – on the broad social consequences of the provision of services in general rather than upon the personal service orientation of professionalism ...

The 'authoritative' pronouncement common under a system of professionalism gives way to the incorporation of practitioners, as advisers and experts within the context of government decision-making.[31]

This series of quotations raises many interesting points for further discussion. Obviously, not all of Johnson's conclusions concerning the characteristics of an occupation under control through 'state mediation' and aspiring to 'professionalism' apply to teachers. But a good number of them do, or at least prompt an exploration to judge the degree of fit between his predictions and the characteristics of teachers associations. We shall refer to Johnson's argument in other places throughout the book, but it should be borne in mind when we come to examine the historical background to the growth of teacher unionism and especially the role played by the state in fostering a 'professional' identity among teachers.

One of Johnson's conclusions, that state mediation led to 'incorporation' of the occupation into the context of government decision-making is given support by those who looked at teacher unionism from the 'political/pressure group' viewpoint the third category that we noted in our discussion of the literature. Not that there is any conscious reference to Johnson's argument concerning the role of the state – indeed any purposeful activity by the state to weaken the trade union aspects of teacher behaviour would be seen as unnecessary by this group, who adopt a natural history approach to the emergence of teaching as a profession, decry the odd outburst of trade union behaviour, and emphasize the role of the teacher unions as part of the educational sub-government as advisers and experts to be consulted on matters of educational policy.

The Political Theory/Pressure Group Literature

The centrality of the capitalist state does not feature in

this literature. Writers within this framework, either explicitly or implicitly, adopt a pluralist theory of the state which essentially sees power distributed at all levels in society and open to influence by groups of free citizens who come together to achieve a shared purpose. The interests of these groups may conflict, but the outcomes are arrived at through negotiation and compromise which somehow reflects a 'consensus' about society's wishes in a particular area of activity. Pluralism denies the importance of class conflict and the manipulative or coercive role of the state.

Writers within this framework have looked at teacher unions within the broader educational and government context. In the main, they are concerned to explore educational policy making and consider the teacher unions as part of that broader topic. Assumptions inherent in the literature already discussed are also brought to bear here, particularly those assumptions which support the view of professional behaviour defined as responsible and consultative as opposed to union, 'sectional', self-interested activity. Writers within this group view consultative behaviour and strategies for acceptance into partnership by the state as the norm for teacher union activity, and militancy as an uncharacteristic departure from that norm.

Kogan has published several studies of educational policy making which devote some attention to the role of teacher unions, but his lengthiest analysis is made in 'Educational Policy Making, a study of interest groups and Parliament',[32] where he distinguishes between 'sectional' and 'promotional' groups. Sectional groups aim

23

to protect and advance the collective interests of their members, promotional groups advocate some more altruistic cause. Kogan admits that some groups straddle this division between sectional and promotional aims, but concludes that the NUT is characterized by a duality of aims:

> First, plainly, they have a clear trade union role, advancing and negotiating salaries and conditions of work for their members. Secondly the associations are a strong force in creating opinion about the style, organization and content of education ... the NUT inevitably faces ambiguity as between its professional and trade union objectives.[33]

The NUT itself, in its evidence to the House of Commons Expenditure Committee, spells out its combined aims with little hint of ambiguity:[34]

> The Union combines the activities and services of a professional organization and a trade union. It has always considered it essential not only to protect and advance the interests of its members in respect of their salaries, and conditions of service ... , but also to secure the improvement of educational provision and the reform and development of the education system, and to work for the enlargement of educational opportunity ... throughout its history the Union has always played a leading part in the discussion and formulation of all aspects of educational policy.

and, when questioned further by the Committee to expand on the written evidence:

> *Chairman of Expenditure Committee* examining the NUT witnesses:
> ... you mention that the Union combines the activities of a professional organization and a trade union. Do you ever find that these two functions conflict with one another in any way?
>
> *President of NUT* (Mrs Elsie Clayton)
> I do not think so. We are initially . . . a professional organization . . . concerned with the quality of the service we offer, its content and its effects on children . . . , and at the same time we look after our members. This is our trade union aspect.
>
> *General Secretary of NUT* (Mr Fred Jarvis)
> I do not think we ever found any problem about what some people see as a dichotomy. Some people think the positions are mutually exclusive.
>
> *Ex-President of NUT* (Mr Max Morris)
> Every improvement in teachers' conditions is inevitably an improvement in the education of the children in our schools. Equally every improvement in educational conditions within schools improves teachers' conditions. The two things go together like that.

Kogan's idea of ambiguity or conflict between sectional and promotional groups has gained considerable currency, however, and is reflected in his own later work and that of Rene Saran, while general writers on the educational system, like Locke, also refer to it. Kogan also distinguishes between legitimized and non-legitimized groups, in order to arrive at an estimate of a particular group's authority and power.

> The legitimized groups are those which have an accepted right to be consulted by government and local authorities, and by public organizations concerned with education such as universities, before policies are authorized. . . . These interest groups differ, however, from government when they promote and defend the interests of their own members, or when they press the DES to expend or maintain the standards of the education service. . . .
>
> The teachers' associations are not the same as the other legitimized associations in this respect. But even they are more a part of the authorized system than they themselves might recognize. They represent the professionals who run public institutions. They represent heads as well as rank and file teachers; and teachers themselves are, in any event, concerned with the maintenance of a system which carries authority and is part of the social control mechanism. Moreover, the teachers' ultimate managers, chief education officers, are themselves almost, if not quite all, former teachers. So the teachers do not argue for the same position as do industrial trade unions. They also face employers who are elected representatives, with

the backing of those who elect them, rather than private employers. Moreover, the breadth of their membership restricts their ability to be decisive, let alone aggressive. The broader the membership, the less easy it is for them to get agreement on policies other than generalized sectional policies on salaries or working conditions. And even on those points there can be quite sharp internal differences. These characteristics soften their relationships with government though, obviously, they are not equivocally* a part of management.

Thus, Kogan argues that the teacher unions do not stand quite apart from government but have, as Saran[36] puts it, 'half a foot in the executive camp'. Kogan strongly suggests that the teacher unions, in their activities, concentrate on fostering relations with the government based on consensus rather than conflict. Indeed, Kogan's analysis of educational policy making in general depends very largely on the idea of continuity and consensus over a long period of time:

> The British system of the government of education is generally assumed to be strong, largely continuous and consensual in its working and in its assumptions. Many educational and institutional policies remained largely unchanged. . . . Indeed, most of them were inherited from the first of the public education systems at the beginning of the twentieth century. The institutional fabric depended upon interaction between the three main

*Kogan clearly means 'unequivocally'.

sets of agents, central government, local authorities and teachers who both sustained the continuity and produced change.[37]

In a later book Kogan seeks to establish 'how the consensus was broken'. He concludes that it was broken on the basis of several 'conflicts' within the system, particularly over curriculum, equality and standards. Within that context he places the 'increased militancy' of the NUT, and allies this to a decline in its influence:

> But opinion is that the union is no longer as major an influence as it was. It has lost some public respect partly because the 'professional' stance put forward by Sir Ronald Gould has been affected by the sharper Trade Union approach of Max Morris and others. The 1969 strike also showed it was as much a trade union as a professional association. And this it confirmed by following the NAS into the TUC.[38]

Locke is one of the many writers on the general educational system who has followed Kogan in dividing the activities of the NUT into two distinct spheres – those where they share a common interest with the DES and local authorities over educational issues, and those where differences arise over pay and working conditions.

Locke also follows Kogan in giving much higher priority to the educational issues, and analyses the strategies employed by the union in pursuit of educational aims in terms of deputations, lobbying publicity campaigns, contacts with officials and ministers.

> The productive work, such as the friendly relations of the DES and the major unions, is done on a day to day basis between officials. With the unions attempting to assist the DES and the Secretary of State to create a climate of opinion in which sufficient resources can be obtained – i.e. the unions operate in partnership with the DES in order to convince Treasury and Cabinet.[39]

Locke also stresses the NUT's lack of party political involvement (using Roy as his source) and contrasts this and the union's responsible behaviour with its changed behaviour – i.e. its militant activity over pay. This militancy, in Locke's opinion, produced a profound split in the union.

> The Executives and leaderships (except in the NAS) have maintained their respectability in order to maintain their educational influence, and agreed only reluctantly to militant action. Younger teachers, and, in the NUT the Rank and File, have argued that militant action was not only necessary on pay but that stronger union action was required on other topics not so much to come to an agreement with central government and local authorities as to force their hand.[40]

So far we have isolated two features of work within this category which have occurred earlier in our review – the acceptance (indeed the affirmation) of a conflict between professionalism and trade unionism, expressed here as a conflict between sectional and promotional aims, and the assumption that professional behaviour is the norm from which unions have recently deviated in outbreaks of militancy.

In addition there is the interesting relationship argued by Kogan to have existed between the unions and the other 'controllers' of the system at central and local level, based on a broad consensus about general educational aims, but rudely shattered by the disillusionment with education widespread in the late 1970s. Such a consensus of central government, local authorities and teachers is often referred to elsewhere in the literature – where it becomes the 'three estates' in education, the 'triangle of tension', the 'triangle of confidence and co-operation', the 'friendly conspiracy', the 'educational sub-government' etc.

What interests us is that in this literature little attention is given to analysing the role of the dominant partner, the state, in fostering this consensus and encouraging the partnership. How could such a literature be reinterpreted using Johnson's and Larson's views of the relationship between the capitalist state and state professionalism?

One study that fits into this general category but which attempts to explain teacher union behaviour in terms of changing strategies in response to central government is Coates' *Teacher Unions and Interest Group Politics*.[41] Coates, like Kogan, details a set of strategies adopted by the union to pursue its educational aims. He, like Kogan sees these as 'professional' strategies, consistently developed over a long period. But, he maintains, changing circumstances – primarily economic – forced the union to change its strategies in order to accommodate to changes in the way government itself operated. The growth of inflation and consequent development of an incomes policy undermined the value of the teachers' relationship with the DES, as *its* freedom of manoeuvre was severely curtailed by the treasury. Accordingly, the teacher unions looked for an alliance with organized labour as a way of securing involvement in national salary agreements and as a way of bringing pressure to bear on central government and the Treasury.

As far as it goes, Coates makes a convincing case, and he must be given credit for not viewing 'interest group' strategies as diametrically opposed to 'professional' aims – the differences for him are essentially tactical, arising from the union's perception of changed circumstances. But his explanation is almost entirely focused on changes within central government, and does not address itself to the problem of how the union itself changed tactics, how the membership contributed to this changed behaviour, and why some strategies, rather than others, were successfully adopted. Coates himself argues that the behaviour of the NUT can be explained in terms of leadership behaviour:

> For with the exception of periods of mass militancy, the behaviour considered here has involved only leadership behaviour in associations in which the existence of formally democratic processes of internal government still leaves (as in most unions)

> immense freedom of action to the executive com-
> mittees and to full-time officer.[42]

This is not really very satisfactory, particularly as 'militancy' forms a central theme of the study, epitomising
Coates' argument that teachers have adapted their
behaviour to fit changed circumstances.

Coates' study is valuable in that it rejects the idea of a
natural partnership between the government, the local
authorities and the teachers which had evolved gradually
and operated through an unshakeable consensus based
on achieving agreed if unstated educational aims. Coates'
study of the NUT as an interest group and his emphasis
on tactics offers a more fruitful way of explaining current
teacher politics than Kogan's later work which is little
more than a lament for the lost consensus and a con-
demnation of teachers' materialism.

Where we disagree with Coates is in his assumption
that the 1960s mark a point of departure from 'half a
century of professional exclusiveness'. We feel that it
would be interesting and useful to pursue his analysis
of union tactics back through the unions' history. It is
also necessary to investigate the ways in which the
membership contributes to changes in strategy, and the
relationship between leadership behaviour and membership behaviour. While we agree that a change in central
government strategy will lead to a tactical change in
NUT behaviour, we argue that this was not a new
departure in the 1960s, and that more investigation into
union initiatives in altering the rules of the game is
required. This in turn calls into question the validity of

the notion of the 'partnership', not just for the present time, but as a characterization of state-teacher-employer relationships since the nineteenth century.

In sum, then, the literature within the pressure group framework depends very heavily on an assumption of consensus about educational aims and a commitment to a pluralist analysis of society in which class conflict and power relations are not important or controversial issues. There is also a heavy bias towards an idea of professionalism which is very much that advanced by the state as an ideology of control – i.e. it is defined as involving responsible behaviour, consultation, concern for standards etc. and achieves its ends through the power of convincing argument. This definition is taken completely at its face value, to the extent that behaviour which falls outside this range is defined as unprofessional, and a decline in influence, if it is indulged in is assumed. Such a limited and divisive view of organized teacher behaviour has stimulated many articles and, more seriously, greatly handicapped a more flexible and dynamic approach.

Summary and Conclusions

In the review of the literature we have attempted to bring out similarities in approaches to the study of teacher unionism and call into question some of the dominant assumptions which underlie those similarities. Histories of teacher unionism have created an image of consistent movement towards professionalism, an image which at once reflects and supports the 'natural history' approach to the professions. This concentration on progress towards professionalism has resulted in an under-emphasis on contradictory or ambiguous actions on the part of teachers, not only among their historians, but among those authors writing about the unions' present status as part of the educational sub-government. Because they assume a history of consistent 'professionalism', the salary campaigns or sanction implementations in support of improved working conditions are considered to be eruptions of untypical militancy and to represent an alteration in union tactics which threatens the existence of educational government based on partnership.

The acceptance of the idea that teachers pursued professional status has had other consequences; union strategies are assumed to be contradictory to the dominant professional ethic, and thus result in ambiguity or conflict in the unions' aims, individual members are assumed to experience a tension between union demands and professional client-centred duties, and the Executive is assumed to suffer conflict with its militant membership and to have lost influence within the consensus-based educational sub-government. It is also assumed that the union has lost public support because of its departure from professional behaviour.

While not denying that organized teachers have pursued strategies which would be described in common sense terms – and indeed, by the NUT itself – as strengthening its professional status, we would like to explore the areas of union activity which have been neglected because of the dominance of the professionalization model and to reject the existence of a necessary dichotomy between 'professional' and 'union' behaviour. The difficulty of arriving at a definition of what constitutes 'professionalism' has been dealt with. The idea of professionalism as a form of occupational control – as outlined by Johnson – would allow a student of union tactics to make greater sense of different strategies pursued by the NUT in response to the state than the assumption of an inherent conflict within the union, with the forces of professionalism triumphant until the 1960s (despite the odd foray from the unionists in the decade 1910–20) but beaten down by the militant anti-professionals in the 60s and 70s. Indeed Johnson's introduction of the notion of state mediation as a form of occupational control leads us to examine the promotional role of the State in fostering a professional consciousness among teachers during the formative years of the union and co-opting the NUT into the sub-government. Such a strategy has permitted the myth of the autonomy of the British teacher to take root and flourish, and may have effectively inhibited direct confrontations between teachers and the state.

We believe that an investigation of teacher union behaviour which takes professionalism to operate as an ideology – chiefly for the benefit of the state in denying class conflict and permitting the manipulation and co-option of teachers but also, because of its contradictory and ambiguous residual elements of autonomy and service, if taken in conjunction with an examination of state mediation and its consequences – would throw more light on teachers than a sterile polarization of professionalism and unionism.

A further factor which must be taken into account when examining organized teachers and their relation

35

Teachers, Professionalism and Class

to the state is the class position of teachers and we now
devote our attention to this.

References

1 THOMPSON, D.F. (1927) *Professional Solidarity Among the Teachers of England*, Colum-
  bia University Press; TROPP, A. (1957) *The School Teachers*, Heinemann; ROY, W.
  (1968) *The Teacher's Union*, Schoolmaster Publications; GOSDEN, P.H.J.H. (1972)
  The Evolution of a Profession, Basil Blackwell.
2 TROPP, A. (1957) *op. cit.*
3 ROY, W. (1968) *op. cit.*, p. 30.
4 TIPTON, B. (1974) 'The hidden side of teaching: The teacher unions', *London
  Educational Review*, Vol. 3, No. 2.
5 TROPP, A. (1957) *op. cit.*
6 THOMPSON, D.F. (1927) *op. cit.*
7 *Ibid.*, p. 82.
8 *Ibid.*, p. 45.
9 *Ibid.*, p. 216.
10 WEBB, B. (1915) 'English teachers and their professional organizations', *New
   Statesman*, (Special Supplements) 25 September and 2 October.
11 *Ibid.*, p. 5.
12 *Ibid.*, p. 11.
13 WEBB, B. and WEBB, S. (1897) *The New Industrial Democracy*, Kelley.
14 WEBB, B. (1915) *op. cit.*
15 MILLERSON, G. (1964) *The Qualifying Associations*, Routledge and Kegan Paul.
16 CARR-SAUNDERS, A.M. and WILSON, P.A. (1933) *The Professions*, Clarendon Press.
17 JOHNSON, T.J. (1972) *Professions and Power*, Macmillan.
18 LARSON, M.S. (1977) *The Rise of Professionalism: A Sociological Analysis*, University
   of California Press.
19 FLEXNER, A. (1915) *Is Social Work a Profession?* (Proceedings of the National
   Conference of Charities and Correction), Hildman Publishing.
20 PARRY, N. and PARRY, J. (1974) 'The teachers and professionalism: The failure of
   an occupational sociology', in FLUDE, M. and AHIER, J. (Eds.) *Educability, Schools
   and Ideology*, Croom Helm.
21 *Ibid.*, p. 160.
22 *Ibid.*, p. 161.
23 *Ibid.*, p. 183.
24 *Ibid.*, p. 183.
25 *Ibid.*, p. 160.
26 *Ibid.*, p. 183.
27 JOHNSON, T.J. (1972) *op. cit.*
28 *Ibid.*, p. 45.
29 *Ibid.*, p. 77.
30 LARSON, M.S. (1977) *op. cit.*
31 JOHNSON, T.J. (1972) *op. cit.*, p. 80.

32 KOGAN, M. (1975) 'Educational policy making: A study of interest groups and Parliament',
33 *Ibid.*
34 House of Commons Expenditure Committee.
35 KOGAN, M. (1975) *op. cit.*
36 SARAN, R. (1979) 'The policy making process in the education system: Pressures on central and local government', (Unit 6 of E222), *The Control of Education in Britain*, Open University Press.
37 KOGAN, M. (1975) *op. cit.*
38 *Ibid.*
39 LOCKE, M. (1974) *Power and Politics in the School System*, Routledge and Kegan Paul.
40 *Ibid.*
41 COATES, R.D. (1972) *The Teacher Unions and Interest Group Politics*, Cambridge University Press.
42 *Ibid.*

Chapter 2.
Teachers and Class

In the preceding chapter we attempted to expose some
of the limitations imposed on much of the literature
concerning organized teachers by the concept of professionalism being inadequately understood and incorrectly
defined. We showed how the mythology of professionalism
led some writers to neglect alternative aspects and
interpretations of organized teacher union history and
behaviour. Above all, we attempted to argue that professionalism may have meant different things to the teachers
and their employers, and that these meanings might have
a strategic importance, also that changes in the meaning
of professionalism could best be understood in relation to

changes in the nature of capitalism and the development of the capitalist state.

There are strong links between the concept of professionalism and 'middle-classness' in the sociology of occupations; indeed, professional status is often used as the defining factor which results in middle class status for the occupation under scrutiny. Looked at more closely, there appear to be three major factors isolated in this literature which are taken to connote both middle class and professional status: a strong market position (for the particular professional skill); a considerable degree of autonomy in the workplace (especially by comparison with the industrialized proletariat); and 'high status'.

For the same reasons that we find most of the literature on professions lacking – i.e. that it takes little account of professionalism as an ideology manipulated by the State, or of the changing nature of capitalism, or of alterations in the meaning of 'professionalism' itself in response to those changes – we find such analysis of class lacking. We agree with Rosemary Crompton's[1] assertion that status, workplace autonomy and market position are all dependent upon and follow from the true determinant of class position; the antagonistic relations of production under capitalism. We can do no better than to reproduce Crompton's summary of the essential features of Marx's account of the structure of the capitalist mode of production:

i   two functions dominate the capitalist mode of production (a) the capitalist function and (b) the labour function. The capitalist function owns or controls the material means of production, and, in addition, owns or controls the labour power 'voluntarily' surrendered by the labour function. Labour, on the other hand, neither owns nor controls productive property (i.e. capital) and, being propertyless, has no alternative but to sell its labour power to the capitalist.

ii Capitalist relations of production are exploitative. New values (as opposed to market values) can only be created through the interaction of labour and the material means of production. The new values necessary to reproduce labour (i.e. to sustain the worker and his family) can be created through working a certain number of hours. These hours Marx termed 'necessary labour time'. This 'surplus labour' like 'necessary labour' creates new values i.e. surplus value, which is neither owned nor controlled by labour but is legally appropriated by the capitalist function.

iii Both labour and capital are essential to the capitalist mode of production. The costs of production of labour are met through the values created by labour. There must, in addition, be assured a continuing supply of capital. Capital, as new values, is created by labour, but is appropriated by the capitalist as surplus value. In order that the capitalist mode of production may continue, the capitalist function must appropriate and accumulate new values as surplus values. Continual pressures towards accumulation are, therefore, inherent in the capitalist mode of production.[2]

The social division of labour is exploitative, integral to it are the antagonistic relations of production which condition social class formation. Adopting this as our basic premise, the task of this section is to explore the ways in which Marxist and neo-Marxist writers have dealt with the social class location of teachers. Obviously teachers constitute a group of workers who do not fall readily into the category of labour in the same unequivocal way as workers on assembly lines in factories do. By the same token, it is clear that teachers are not themselves capitalists, owning and controlling the means of production, and appropriating surplus value from labour. Nor are teachers the only workers who present difficulties in terms of class location – there are problems in locating many service workers and white collar workers. The relative numerical growth of this sector of the population has led to much non-Marxist work on the 'new middle classes', which postulates a decline in the traditional middle class and the growth of a new sector, which itself bears a close resemblance to the bureaucratised professional group identified by sociologists of the professions.

However, within Marxist analysis too, the idea of a middle class, either emerging as a new class or as a revised and altered version of the petty bourgeoisie, has taken a strong hold in much recent writing. Again the impetus behind much of this writing seems to come from the growth in white collar and service industry, and in the number of State personnel. There are obvious difficulties in fitting these personnel into the classic Marxist formulation. Obviously, the idea of a 'middle' class, positioned between the proletariat and the bourgeoisie, has considerable consequences for a Marxist analysis and the discussion of a new class is a controversial and complex one. In addition, little work has concerned itself directly with teachers, though they are sometimes referred to as part of the 'State personnel' group of workers.

We have therefore tried to extrapolate from the current debate those points which seem to us to be relevant to teachers. However, we cannot simply isolate these points, they have to be placed within the general context of the debate within Marxism concerning the question of a 'middle class'. Without attempting to summarize that debate, which would be an impossibly complex and lengthy task, it is still necessary to examine the major points at issue while looking specifically at the teachers. There is a grave danger here that, in simplifying the debate for our own purposes, we may do less than justice to the complexity of the discussion and to the subtlety of some of the positions held by individuals. This is particularly true of arguments at a very high level of abstraction which we attempt to bring down to the practical level and apply to a group of workers. On the other hand, if no attempt is ever made to bridge the gulf between theoretical discussion and the objective conditions of groups of workers, then the discussion itself may lose much of its value.

We look then, firstly, at what may broadly be called the economic determinants of class location, the classic Marxist formulation, as summarized by Crompton, and some of the debate on productive and unproductive labour. Next we examine that strand of Marxist analysis which regards education as playing a role vital to capitalism in the reproduction of the labour force, and which defines education as part of an ideological state apparatus and teachers as the 'professional ideologues of capitalism'. This issue is raised by the question of the importance of political and ideological determinants of class position, and we assess the consequences of analysing teachers class position in these terms.

The Primacy of the Economic?

A fairly basic approach to class definition within the Marxist framework has been to apply the simple criteria of control over the means of production and sale of labour power. Hence Ginsberg, Meyenn and Miller,[3] in a discussion of teachers' class position, assert that teachers are not capitalists but wage earners because they sell their labour power and neither own nor control the means of production. This, as they recognize, avoids the fundamental issue of production of surplus value, i.e. while teachers may be exploited in terms of the sale of their labour power, they do not produce surplus value which is appropriated by the capitalist and are, hence, not productive workers. Ginsberg, Meyenn and Miller go on to make this point, and to develop it – if teachers do not produce surplus value but are paid out of the surplus value produced by other (exploited) workers, are teachers themselves exploiters? Ginsberg, Meyenn and Miller resolve their dilemna by locating teachers in an ambivalent class location, neither workers nor capitalists, but members of the 'new middle class', sometimes sympathetic to the working class but exploiting it economically and oppressing it ideologically.

This article neatly brings together all the strands within Marxist and neo-Marxist thought which will concern us, and ties them together to assign teachers to an 'ambivalent' middle class location. A major factor in determining that allocation from an economic point of view is the definition of the teacher as an unproductive worker, paid out of surplus value produced by others. This is seen to cancel out the exploitation of teachers through the sale of their labour power.

The question of the productive and unproductive labourer has proved an enormously problematic one for Marxists attempting to establish the boundaries of working class membership. On the face of it, following Marx, a great many workers who do not produce surplus value should appear to face exclusion from the working class. Yet at the same time, anomalies appear as a consequence of rigid application of this distinction; to use the Ehrenreichs' example, a supermarket assistant who stacks shelves, and thus participates in the final stages of commodity production, is part of the working class, while the colleague who operates the till is not. An even stranger anomaly to those working in English State Schools is the working class location of the schoolteacher who sells his/her labour to a private school proprietor. In Marx's words:

If we may take an example from outside the

> sphere of production of material objects, a school-
> master is a productive labourer when, in addition
> to belabouring the heads of his scholars, he works
> like a horse to enrich the school proprietor. That
> the latter has laid out his capital in a teaching
> factory, instead of a sausage factory, does not alter
> the relation.[4]

How do we deal with these anomalies? One strategy is to
relax the rigid adherence to the production of surplus
value as defining the productive worker. Hunt, for
example, argues that insufficient attention has been paid
to the development of capital since Marx produced his
analysis. As capitalism has become increasingly sophisticated, so the growth of bureaucracy and service functions
has proceeded. More is produced in the form of invisible
commodity, rather than material commodity, and more
of capital devoted to such industries. 'State revenue
expenditure on – for example, health and education –
is an increasingly important component of real wages
and, as such, the labour expended can be regarded as
contributing to the reproduction of variable capital'.

Rosemary Crompton[5] also develops a similar argument, based on the role of workers in state and service
industries – white collar workers in banking, insurance
and commercial sectors, for example. The argument is
that such workers play a role vital to capitalism through
their role in the *realization* of surplus value. Their importance lies in the sphere of circulation. Not only is
their role in circulating capital vital to capital, the process
of realization, itself, introduces new mechanisms of control

46

which watch over and enlarge capital. Thus, in Johnson's words:

> The concentration of capital makes for greater complexity in this process whereby the realization function of capital is itself transformed into a labour process (albeit unproductive). There has, then, emerged a labour process – a vast body of people producing nothing but increasingly elaborate control mechanisms for the realization and enlargement of capital. ... The labour process which develops in the implementation of these systems of control is subjected to the same forms of coercive control as are constituted in the direct appropriation of surplus value, but are here subordinated to a process of realization rather than appropriation.[6]

Thus, one suggested development is that state employees contribute to the reproduction of variable capital and this may be seen as productive, another stresses the growth and importance of the realization of surplus value and the exploitative relationship of control pertaining in that sphere, as in the sphere of surplus value appropriation. Both arguments contribute to the case for regarding the distinction between unproductive and productive labour as defining the economic identification of the working class as, at the very least, problematic.

A further factor linked to both of these arguments is the development of the 'collective labourer'. Marx predicted the gradual breakdown of work into its component parts and the erosion of the worker's control over the labour process by means of this division. The emergence of monopoly capitalism has led to this process characterising all forms of work, with ever-increasing differentiation and specialisation. Marx's term 'collective labourer' i.e. the group brought together to produce a commodity, can now, because of changes and developments in non-material production, be applied to many workers outside the industrial sphere. This extension of the 'collective labourer' means that many workers, hitherto regarded as unproductive when functioning independently, become productive workers as part of the collective labourer:

> As the co-operative character of the labour-process becomes more and more marked, so, as a necessary consequence, does our notion of productive labour, and of its agent the productive labourer, become extended.[7]

However, these qualifications are fairly muted by comparison with the literature of those (including Carchedi and Poulantzas) who, faced with the growth of white-collar, supervisory 'non-productive' workers, have felt it necessary to assign these workers to a middle class. In Carchedi's[8] terms, a new middle class; for the Ehrenreichs,[9] a new 'professional middle class' and for Poulantzas,[10] a radically revised version of the petty bourgeoisie.

As we have seen, the arguments concerning economic determination of social class are complex, though their application has often been crude particularly when a rigid application of the productive/non-productive labourer distinction has been used to define workers out of the working class (as in the Ginsberg, Meyenn and Miller article). Faced with a dwindling working class as a consequence of such rigid economism, yet uneasily aware that these problematic workers are not readily assigned to the ruling class, the concept of a new middle class affords a convenient way out of the immediate dilemma, though its use, as we hope to demonstrate, obscures rather than develops our understanding of class.

In addition to the problems discussed above, there are good grounds for rejecting a rigid distinction between productive and unproductive labour as a basis for economic class determination. As Hunt[11] argues, 'any fundamental criteria for class determination must reveal real differences between the classes and their members' – yet the unproductive/productive distinction imposes an arbitary division between workers sharing important common characteristics: they are exploited (through the extraction of their labour); they have antagonistic relations with their employers; the value of their labour power is determined in the same way; and, finally, the labour of the unproductive worker, it can be suggested, is as necessary to capital as that of the productive worker. Can they therefore be said to belong to different, and therefore opposed, classes?

Do we then need to look beyond the economic determinants of class to establish class location? Certainly, in the work of theorists of the new middle class the relationship between political, ideological and economic factors is prominent. Nor would we ourselves wish to suggest that class location is simply economically determined,

classes are sets of social relations, but these relations draw
their character from the antagonistic relations of production. The precise nature of the relationship between the
political, the ideological and the economic or technical
determinants of class location presents enormous problems. Hunt[12] suggests that 'the economic level of the
technical relations of production prescribes the parameters
or outer boundaries of class structures ... political and
ideological practices have the effect of establishing the
relation of the participants to classes. These practices
can be conceived as "linking" or "tying" the participants
to a class; and on the other hand of "separating" or
"distancing" them from another class location'.

Yet in the analysis of a new middle class, this relationship has been either rendered obscure or has been reduced
to a form which very nearly reproduces the work of
non-Marxist class theoreticians, with its invocations of a
mental/manual divide, its stress on supervisory functions
and its use of vague criteria such as 'common life style'
to establish class identity. Let us look more closely at the
ideological and political determinants of the new middle
class.

Politics and Ideology – The Ambivalent Middle Class

In Carchedi's terms, the new middle class consists of those
who carry out the global functions of capital (control
and surveillance) while also carrying out the functions of
the collective labourer, it is a class which

does not own either legally or economically the
means of production ... performs both the global
functions of capital and the function of the collective worker ... it is therefore both the labourer
(productive and unproductive) and the non-
labourer and ... is both exploiter (or oppressor)
and exploited (or oppressed).[13]

Poulantzas' new petty bourgeoisie is also caught in an
ambivalent or contradictory class location. Having argued
that the political and ideological do not act as variables
added to pre-existing economic relations but operate to
determine those relations and to sanction the exploitative
relations of production, Poulantzas separates his new
petty bourgeoisie from the proletariat in all three spheres.
Workers, in Poulantzas' terms, are economically defined
by direct involvement in material commodity production,
a statement which theoretically reduces the working class
to a near-minority in most advanced capitalist societies.

In the political sphere the social relations of production
dictate the domination by supervisors of productive
workers to ensure the extraction of surplus value. Supervisors, therefore, and all who engage in controlling work
processes, are part of the new petty bourgeoisie. At the
ideological level Poulantzas makes much of a mental/
manual division between the working class and other
classes. For example, white collar workers dominate the
working class because of their expert knowledge which
they do not share with other workers.

In relation to our enquiry into teachers, Poulantzas'
discussion of ideology is important. Indeed, much of his

new petty bourgeoisie appears to be located within the State as members of one or other function of the State apparatus, whereby the State, acting as the agent of capitalism, prevents the working class from acquiring State power and hegemony. Education, as an ideological State apparatus, reproduces the labour force necessary for capitalism and inculcates in the working class the attitudes necessary for capitalism's continuation.

Thus, the new petty bourgeoisie, which includes teachers and other State personnel, is differentiated economically, politically and ideologically from the working class. However, it is not internally linked but fragmented and fractionalised, due to its contradictory and stressful location; caught between the bourgeoisie above (where the upper echelons of the State apparatus are apparently located) and the proletariat below.

Because of the proximity to the working class, particularly in the lower echelons of the State apparatus, popular struggles within that class also affect the new petty bourgeoisie and there are relationships both of conflict and alliance between the new petty bourgeoisie and the working class. However, the new petty bourgeoisie is held in loyalty to the State by the dominant ideology which presents the State as a neutral representative of the general aim and interest, an arbiter above and beyond class interests. But the 'ideological sub-ensembles' within the apparatus are often interpreted by sections of the State personnel as defining their duty to establish social justice and 'equality of opportunity' among citizens.

Agents of the State personnel who go over to the

side of the popular masses often live their revolt in terms of the dominant ideology ... thus even sections of the state personnel which go over to the popular masses do not challenge the reproduction of the social division of labour within the state apparatus (i.e. the processes of bureaucratisation and hierarchization) nor, *a fortiori*, do they normally challenge the political division between rulers and ruled that is embodied in the state.[14]

Poulantzas' new petty bourgeoisie, then, appears to be located ambivalently apart from the working class, primarily because of its ideological committment (to the state, in the case of state personnel) and because it is not engaged in material production. Yet, in any attempt to bring his abstract discussion down to the level of workers in specific situations, enormous problems present themselves. Leaving aside the question of material production (which does not seem to have a basis in Marx's writings) the statement that alliances may be formed with the working class by the lower echelons of the new petty bourgeoisie but that these alliances are partial because of the strength of state ideology, raises more questions than it answers. How, for example, does Poulantzas establish that a social worker, engaged in sympathetic industrial action with other workers, does not question his function within the ideology of the state apparatus? Surely, at this level of the new petty bourgeoisie, the line of demarcation becomes very blurred indeed. Nor does the invocation of a mental/manual division help us particularly as the introduction of technology removes control of the work

Teachers, Professionalism and Class

process from mental and manual labourer alike.

The Ehrenreichs,[15] in their identification of a 'professional middle class', are closest to the approach within the conventional sociology of the professions which we criticised at the outset of this chapter, and it is difficult to avoid the feeling that what is presented is a conventional 'new middle class' thesis with some Marxist terminology added. The 'professional middle class' consists of technical, managerial workers and 'creative producers' who make up a new class, 'defined by its relation to the economic structure' (presumably by living off surplus value produced by others) and by 'a common life style, a coherent social and cultural existence'. It is interesting to note, especially in relation to the questions raised above about the lower echelons of Poulantzas' state personnel, that the Ehrenreichs too have problems with boundary maintenance. The professional middle class shades off into the working class (like professions shading off into semi-professions) when the occupations in question are dominated by women who are not only assumed to take on the social class of their husbands (thereby rendering antagonistic class relations resolvable through marriage) but who have been de-skilled and proletarianized.

In sum, the further we move in discussing the political and ideological components of the various new middle classes the closer we come to the arguments used by sociologists of the professions to ascribe professional status to certain occupations and deny it to others – the possession of knowledge, the high status/shared lifestyle, the absence of female membership, the acceptance of the political *status quo*.

54

A further problem, as we have already indicated, is that of the 'ambivalence' of the class location. When this is combined with a separation of the political, the ideological and the economic as defining factors in class analysis the ambivalence of middle class location becomes even greater. For Olin Wright,[16] it is elevated to a state of permanent contradiction. He, for example, places teachers at the level of production relations between the petty bourgeoisie and the working class and, at the ideological level, between the bourgeoisie and the working class. Teachers are thus simultaneously located between the working class and the petty bourgeoisie and the working class and the bourgeoisie.

> This disarticulation between their class location at the economic and ideological levels has important consequences for the political role of teachers in class struggle. To the extent that teachers have a certain real level of autonomy at the level of the social relations of (educational) production, they can potentially subvert bourgeois ideology at the level of ideological relations. They are thus in potential contradiction as, despite proletariariza- tion at the economic level, they remain in con- tradiction between the bourgeoisie and the pro- letariat at the ideological level. Teachers, then, occupy objectively contradictory locations within class locations.[17]

This assumption, like Poulantzas' relies heavily on the importance of the ideological determinant for teachers

Teachers, Professionalism and Class

(and other state employees who may be proletarianized at the economic level). Teachers are presumably located between the bourgeoisie and the proletariat at the ideological level because of the role they play in operating an ideological state apparatus, teaching workers, distributing life chances and implanting beliefs in the working class which permit capitalism to survive. The assumption that teachers operate in this way lies behind the importance given to the ideological factor when assessing their class location and there are many separate points of origin which support the notion of teachers as agents of social control, both within and outside Marxist sociology, which may be brought together to support the argument – Bernstein, for example, has written of teachers as 'that fraction of the middle class who function as agents of cultural reproduction',[18] while Althusser's[19] identification of an ideological state apparatus, and Bowles and Gintis'[20] thesis on the relationship between education and the replication of the social relations necessary for capitalism, have further strengthened the case for teachers' exclusion from the working class on ideological grounds. The idea of the middle-class, ambiguous, contradictorily located teacher, possibly proletarianized at the economic level, but acting (wittingly or unwittingly) as an ideological oppressor of the working class, is on the way to becoming orthodox belief among Marxist and neo-Marxist sociologists of education.

For example, Finn, Grant and Johnson,[21] in one of the few extended attempts to grapple with the class location of teachers, draw on various parts of the discussion so far. Firstly, in relation to surplus value:

56

The school is not characterized by the appropriation of surplus value and by capitalist relations in
the classical sense

although it plays a crucial role in the production of labour
power, and

teachers are not proletarians, they are unproductive workers.[22]

In addition, class is not merely defined economically,
but in political and ideological terms. According to Finn,
Grant and Johnson, teachers have used their professional
status and expertise to distance themselves from the
working class.

teaching has been ideologically constructed to
emphasize differences from the working class.[23]

Yet again, the idea of professionalism as a strategy used
by teachers against the working class is invoked; and tied
to their assigned petty-bourgeois class allocation.

Trapped between the developing power of monopoly capitalism and the advances of the working
class, professionalism can be understood as a petty
bourgeois strategy for advancing and preserving a
relatively privileged position.[24]

So finally then, we are left with a conceptual rap-
prochement between sociologists who see themselves as

operating within a Marxist framework, and those historians and sociologists of occupations who have seen professionalism as a strategy for upward mobility. In a separate section we have discussed the different meanings of professionalism as a strategy to employer and employee and its changing meanings in changing contexts. Let us now attempt a similar critical exercise on the 'new middle class' position assigned to teachers. It may be helpful to summarise the main points of argument and our disagreement with them under separate headings:

(i) The question of the distinction between productive and unproductive labour and its use as a means of defining class location

Basically, in addition to all the arguments, outlined above, relating to surplus value realization and the role of state employees in reproducing variable capital, which suggest that a rigid adherence to surplus value production based exclusively on material production and excluding white collar work takes insufficient account of the development of monopoly capitalism, we suggest that :

a Productive and unproductive workers are more united by their common exploitation and their fundamentally antagonistic relations with their employers than divided by the technical application of the criteria of surplus value production. There is no convincing case for antagonistic class relations between such workers on this basis alone.

b The emphasis on the economic as *the* structural determining factor represents a fundamental underuse of
the relational nature of class, i.e. the extent to which
classes are not 'things' but sets of social relations,
characterized by the anatagonistic nature of that
relation: 'The separate individuals form a class only
in so far as they have to carry on a common battle
against another class' . . . we shall return to this point
later.

(ii) The question of a new middle class

The existence of a (new) middle class depends to a large
extent on adherence to a rigid demarcation between
productive and unproductive work, and to the assumption
that the growing group of 'unproductive' workers are in
some sense political and ideological oppressors of the
working class. This assumption rests on the notion of a
division between mental and manual labour (again, a
distinction not made by Marx). How convincing is this
supposed antagonistic relation? If we accept that the
distinction at the economic level is untenable, does this
necessarily force us in the direction of a 'new class' because
of the ideological/political division? The authors we have
discussed fall back on 'ambivalence' and 'contradictory'
class locations to disguise the lack of clear differentiation
of this middle class from the working class. Again, we
would argue that their common interests outweigh their
differences and that it is not necessary to assume, as
Poulantzzs does, that employment within a state apparatus inhibits the development of antagonistic relations

59

with the employer and rejection of state ideology. There are other, more fruitful ways of exploring the contradictions and conflicts of white collar and state personnel rather than through the creation of a new 'middle class' in which they are permanently and pointlessly caught between proletarianisation and embourgeoisement.

(iii) The structural location of class – disembodied structuralism?

This final point really sums up our disagreement with much of the work that we have discussed, and the place of teachers within it. We have hinted at it in stressing the relational aspects of class as discussed by Marx and in drawing on Hunt's attempt to bring together the economic, political and ideological factors and the interaction between them as a dynamic process. Much of the Marxist and neo-Marxist writing discussed above also professes to explore the relationship between these three factors but, on closer scrutiny, seems to us to come very close to a crude economism (which divides the 'middle class' from productive workers) plus a highly subjective analysis, very similar to that present in non-Marxist sociology, which is little more than a descriptive list of ascribed middle class characteristics. We have already discussed the problem of accepting that state personnel must accept the dominant ideology of the state and are, therefore, ideological oppressors of the working class but the assumption that supervisory work activity is inevitably politically oppressive of the working class seems to us equally questionable.

None of this writing draws on any evidence about the

objective work situation of 'problematic' white collar workers and state personnel. Because the analysis takes place at such a high level of abstraction, sweeping assumptions are made – particularly about the political and ideological activities of the 'new middle class' – which we feel do not take sufficient account of changes in the objective nature of white collar work, nor do these assumptions allow for change and development among the white collar workers under discussion. The abstract discussion is not located within any specific historical context, the boundaries of class are immutably fixed, and the notion of change and struggle within and between classes assigned a secondary importance.

Yet an analysis of the location of the class situation of white collar workers and state employees, which embraced the economic, ideological and political level and the interaction between them, must take into account their changing role within the labour process, partly through historical analysis, and partly through an understanding of their proletarianisation. However, such an analysis must also take into account the connected changes in the political and ideological practice among such workers – foremost among them being their increased trade union activity – which we believe cannot be dismissed as the temporary alliance of the lower echelons of the petty bourgeoisie with the working class but demonstrates the growth of working class consciousness at the economic, political and ideological level. Obviously there remain conflicts and contradictions within this group of workers, which includes teachers, but these conflicts are not in themselves sufficient to constitute objective antagonistic class relations and separate these workers, as a class, from the working class.

Nor is it satisfactory to assume that, if education acts as a means of reproducing the labour force by inculcating both skills and attitudes necessary for the continuation of capitalism, then teachers are the witting or unwitting agents of an ideological state apparatus and, hence, oppressors of the working class. Such an argument seems to us tantamount to the suggestion that car assembly workers have an interest in maintaining monopoly capitalism because of their contribution to the profits of major multi-nationals. In any event, the relationship between the function of education as required by the 'state apparatus' and the activities carried out in schools by teachers is a more subtle and complex one, we would suggest, than simple reproduction and indoctrination. Not to recognize this is to ignore teachers' historical struggles for working class education and to embrace a pessimistic determinism which renders teachers and other workers mere social puppets. Teacher organisations, as we hope we have demonstrated, were able to use the ideology of professionalism for their own purposes and did, and do, engage in efforts to change and affect their work content and conditions. Objective analysis of these efforts, particularly as the state moves towards more overt political ideological and economic control over teacher activity, will, we believe, reveal more about the structural class location of teachers than abstract analyses which assure their collaboration with the state.

References

1 CROMPTON, R. (1976) 'Approaches to the study of white collar unionism', *Sociology*, Vol. 10.
2 *Ibid.*, p. 413.
3 GINSBERG, M., MEYENN, R. and MILLER, H. (1980) 'Teachers' conceptions of professionalism and trades unionism: An ideological analysis', in WOODS, P. (Ed.) *Teacher Strategies, Explorations in the Sociology of the School*, Croom Helm.
4 MARX, K. (1869) *Capital*, (Vol. 1), Foreign Language Publishing Co., Moscow, (1961), p. 509.
5 CROMPTON, R. (1976) *op. cit.*
6 JOHNSON, T. (1977) 'What is to be known? The structural determination of social class', *Economy and Society*, Vol. 6.
7 MARX, K. (1961) *op. cit.*, p. 508.
8 CARCHEDI, G. (1975) 'On the economic identification of the new middle class', *Economy and Society*, Vol. 4, No. 1.
9 EHRENREICH, B. and EHRENREICH, J. (1979) 'The professional-managerial class', in WALKER, P. (Ed.) *Between Labor and Capital*, Boston, South End Press.
10 POULANTZAS, N. (1977) 'The new petty bourgeoisie', in HUNT, A. (Ed.) *Class and Class Structure*, Lawrence and Wishart.
11 HUNT, A. (1977) 'Theory and politics in the identification of the working class', in HUNT, A. (Ed.) *Class and Class Structure*, Lawrence and Wishart.
12 *Ibid.*, p. 104.
13 CARCHEDI, G. (1975) *op. cit.*, p. 51.
14 POULANTZAS, N. (1978) *State, Power, Socialism*, New Left Books, p. 154.
15 EHRENREICH, B. and EHRENREICH, J. (1979) *op. cit.*
16 OLIN WRIGHT, E. (1979) 'Intellectuals and the class structure of capitalist society', in WALKER, P. (Ed.) *Between Labor and Capital*, Boston, South End Press.
17 *Ibid.*, p. 208.
18 BERNSTEIN, B. (1975) *Class, Codes and Control*, Vol. 3, Routledge and Kegan Paul.
19 ALTHUSSER, L. (1971) 'Ideology and ideological state apparatuses', in COSIN, B.R. *Education: Structure and Society*, Penguin.
20 BOWLES, S. and GINTIS, H. (1976) *Schooling in Capitalist America*, Routledge and Kegan Paul.
21 FINN, D., GRANT, N. and JOHNSON, R. (1977) 'Social democracy, education and the crisis', *Cultural Studies 10: On Ideology*, Centre for Contemporary Cultural Studies, University of Birmingham.
22 *Ibid.*, p. 170.
23 *Ibid.*
24 *Ibid.*

PART TWO

Chapter 3.
Teachers and White Collar Unionism

We have argued so far that teachers have been unproblematically defined as divided from other workers. Definitions which drew on the ideas of non-productive labour, middle class status-seeking, professionalism or collaboration with the State have all been used, sometimes in combination, to differentiate teachers; that is, to isolate them by means of their assumed ideology, or economic or social location, from other workers. Yet all workers, in our opinion, have similar difficulties depending on their level of political development, their class consciousness, the nature of their work under monopoly capital or the complexities or contradictions of their class position. The determination to classify teachers in ways which do not correspond to at least some of their actions suggests an unwillingness to recognize the ways in which teachers and other workers *share* the same problems.

In this section we will attempt two things: first, an examination of historical evidence which shows that explanatory concepts used in the literature we have reviewed do not reveal the complexity of the situation of teachers nor the consistency of their concern for conditions of work, pay and their resistance to employers; second, we will look at similar problems faced by white collar workers in industry and government services, the contradictions amongst them and the way in which the trend toward proletarianization is not disguised by uneven political development.

Teachers and the Labour Movement

By 1910, the National Union of Teachers had been in existence for forty years, and had grown from a group of 400 teachers to a large union of 68,000 teachers, doubling in size between 1895 and 1910. It had become better and more efficiently organised – with a proper Organising Committee, more and more local Associations (516 in 1910) and executive members responsible for the effectiveness of the Union organisation in different parts of the country. It had a Law Committee, with a full time Union Solicitor, and a Tenure Committee, constantly involved in helping teachers who had been dismissed or were in dispute with Managers or Local Education Authorities.

Low wages were paid to teachers in the rural areas,

especially in the voluntary schools, and women teachers were paid on a lower rate than men in town and country. In the towns and cities, teachers' wages were generally higher, due to the strength and organisation of teachers in their local Associations. In some towns, previous to 1902, the teachers had, in alliance with progressive educational forces, controlled or influenced the local School Boards. They were not, in other words, willing to be seen as mere employees. In rural areas, the influence of the vicar and the farmers was very strong. The rural teacher could be described in 1873 as:

> the mere creature of the clergyman, and he knows it, and so also do both the clergyman and the children know it. Some brawl took place this year between a vicar and a master of his schools. In the course of it, the vicar presumed to write a public letter in which he says, with more truth and boldness than discretion – 'I, not he, am vicar of Dudley; I, not he, am chairman of the managers; and I will not allow him to insult me openly without letting him know that our relative positions are those of master and servant'.[1]

The position of teacher in the rural school was often to include Church duties, such as choirmaster, sexton, organist, Sunday school teacher and even secretarial or tutorial work as well. These were not options but a condition of the livelihood.

By 1910, the National Union of Teachers had already had to support two local associations (Portsmouth in

1896 and West Ham in 1907) in local authority disputes, which involved striking or giving 'notice'. A common factor in both disputes was the Union's attempt to protect teachers' conditions of work when the local authority was encouraged to reduce salaries or alter workloads. Urban authorities were particularly hard pressed financially as their populations increased; the consequent need for services paid for out of rates tended to overwhelm low-rated areas. This was further exacerbated in the early 1900s by the gradual reduction of Exchequer grants to the local authorities.

The Union preferred to operate a local authority employment blacklist where pay and conditions were poor, and advertised on the front page of the *Schoolmaster* asking teachers to refuse jobs in these areas. This tactic was undermined by the number of unemployed or non-Union teachers who were under no obligation to the NUT.

The West Ham dispute occupied several columns in the *Schoolmaster* every week and was obviously felt to be an important example of the increasing local authority pressure on teachers, and teachers reminded themselves and the Executive that it was vital to win the dispute. The West Ham Council was fighting for the right to control its workforce, to get a cheaper system of education and to break the power of the Union; this much is clear from the Council debates published in the local papers. The Union, faced with a local employer ready and willing to import 600 Scottish teachers to break the strike, compromised on the principle of Unionism and the pay scale, much to the disgust of its local supporters, the

Labour Councillors, although the result was widely regarded as a Union victory.

Faced with increasingly hostile local authorities and an indifferent Board of Education (at least, until George Kekewich was Secretary there), the Union needed allies in the fight for an improved elementary education system and a reorganised secondary education. It looked increasingly towards an organised working class in the School Board elections and, later, in national campaigns. The Trades Union Congress policy of a secondary education freely available to all, while more radical than the NUT's policy, could accomodate a joint response to the loss of the pupil teacher centres as an example of the closing of an avenue of further education to the working class. In 1908, an NUT conference resolution on class size made the following point:

> to secure the co-operation of the Trades Congress, Labour Representation Committee, the Independent Labour Party, the Co-operative Societies, Trades Unions and any other organisation interested in the educational welfare of the children to bring about this urgent reform.[2]

This appeal was reproduced in an NUT pamphlet called 'Small Classes and Better Teaching Staff – Help the Worker's Child' in the following year. The alliance with the organised working class was, at the turn of the Century, expressed in educational, not political or economic terms. The serious rise in the rate of inflation (20 per cent between 1901 and 1912) eroded the fixed rate

71

wages of teachers and came to increase the necessity to gain support from the local Trades Councils and Labour councillors. A middle class unwilling to raise the rates, in other words to tax itself, to provide services for the working class was their enemy also.

The teaching profession was also changing in balance and composition. In 1855, most certificated teachers could expect to become headteachers, and yet, by 1895, only 60 per cent could expect to be – by 1918, the figure was 30 per cent. In effect, certification was rapidly devalued and the prospect for certificated teachers was increasingly to be assistants in the school, not heads. If promotion was not available then pressure to change the fixed rate wage was inevitable. Since 1855, there had been a steady rise in the number of uncertificated teachers; in 1879, there were three certificated teachers to every uncertificated one, and in 1899, there were six certificated to five uncertificated teachers. The great majority of the uncertificated teachers, including the 'supplementaries', were women employed at a lower rate than the men. Indeed, the supplementaries (or 'Article 68ers') were qualified merely by being vaccinated and over 18 years of age – they were generally employed in country areas, and their work included looking after the infants and duties including cleaning and fire-lighting. In other words, women were used increasingly as cheap labour in the education system. With their lack of certification, they were ineligible for membership of the NUT and generally existed outside of union organisation. They were also generally single as most authorities sacked women teachers on marriage. The growth of two strong

NUT pressure groups, after 1900, can be traced to the developing composition of the union. The National Federation of Class Teachers was formed in the early 1890's by certificated class teachers and organised around the issue of class teachers' rights. The National Federation of Women Teachers was initially created as an Equal Pay League by male and female teachers but reconstituted itself in 1906 as a pressure group for women's rights and representation in the Union and for equal suffrage.

The London teachers, in this period, were well organised and their documented struggles illustrate the nature of the fight by the teachers for better conditions, their alliance with working class representatives and the constant pressure for improvement in their conditions of work. All teachers struggled with employers: either the local squire, vicar or tradesmen-managers or local authority employers' combinations or the Education Department.

The London teachers had obtained and protected better pupil-teacher ratios than obtained elsewhere (one teacher to fifty pupils as opposed to a national average of one teacher to eighty pupils, in 1899). The teachers were encouraged to become trained and certificated and to add other qualifications on School Management etc. The pupil-teacher centres were centres of teacher excellence – later becoming bases for the new secondary schools.

Yet, until 1893, the School Managers selected the teachers, regularly inspected the teacher's own attendance and punctuality record, and often had special rooms in the school, sometimes even special, reserved staircases, to work from. Even when the School Board created its own inspectors in the early 1880s to organise the schools, examine pupils and check registers, this was seen by teachers as a formalisation of a previously irregular control. The Revised Code and the local School Board businessmen placed the London teachers in a tight grip which they resisted.

The Revised Code had altered the teachers' work and pay. They were increasingly seen as the servants of managers and inspectors; great emphasis was placed on their new clerical duties and their teaching work was narrowly redefined. They were paid partly from commission. Their work was organised within tight timetables, emphasis was placed on measurable results or standards and certain books were prescribed in their work. With the exception of headteachers, who seemed to be increasingly isolated from the other teachers not just by their certification but increasingly by their administrative tasks in the larger schools and their direct share of the government grant, most teachers in London seemed to have had a downward proletarianizing push from their masters. This led to a lack of motivation and interest in their work which was diagnosed by their employers as a failure of duty and led to more compulsory duties which in turn promoted an organised resistance by the teachers.

Teachers regularly protested at the increases in their workload. They were expected, from 1877, to be at school ten minutes before its opening and to be registered in an attendance book. 'Penny Banks' were started in 1873 and continued though teachers resented this extra duty. Clerical duties increased – compulsory attendance registers made in duplicate, schedules and school certificates.

The Education Department regularly produced new suggestions on infections diseases, eyesight tests, cleanliness of pupils and the new dinner duties – most of this new work was checked by the Inspectors. The Metropolitan Board Teachers' Association protested at the compulsory clerical work, which led the Education Department to remark in a report that:

> teachers too often seem to think that since the introduction of compulsion, their duty to children begins and ends with the hours of the timetable.[3]

The Board's own report on Salaries in 1878 used 'duty' as a watchword.

In response to the increased duties and the strong external control placed on their work plus the reduced prospects and wages (and perhaps the pious management hope that 'duty' was sufficient), the teachers organised. The Metropolitan Board Teachers' Association, which had been a 'professional' meeting place, began to act as a union of organised workers. It recruited most of the certificated teachers in the 1890s; moving from forty per cent in 1873 to ninety per cent in the 1900s, which meant about seven thousand teachers. It acted as a regular source and vehicle of complaint on

> salaries, superannuation, promotions, security of tenure, curriculum, staffing ratio and discipline.[4]

The Lambeth and District Teachers' Association had a mass meeting in 1895, which produced a statement that teachers:

> are now occupying more permanent positions,
> with little or no prospect of promotion to headships
> and that the salaries of certificated teachers . . .
> are now quite inadequate.[5]

There is evidence gained from a reading of the London teacher's history to suggest that the State was not the only body concerned with education as the teachers were constantly fighting to protect it against philistine interests; that a combination of controls and 'duty' forced teachers to resist their employers; that unionisation did not involve co-optation but resistance; that teachers were under pressure, as were other members of the working class, to break their craft traditions and abandon control over their work.

In the struggle between teachers and employers, the strategy and tactics employed by one side or the other may change. It is not always clear what the strategies are, as neither side holds consistently to one and they are enmeshed together in a tension created within the employee-employer relationship. At different times, different approaches, representing different groups within the Union leadership, come to the fore. One such was the move for a Teachers' Professional Register.

At the turn of the Century and during its first decade, the National Union of Teachers was under growing pressure from the dilution of the workforce by unskilled (non-certificated) labour. A declining standard of living was felt to result from this dilution. Women teachers were seen, in the main, as cheap unorganised labour, undercutting the craft standards (certification) which had previously controlled work and pay. The Board of Education, which controlled the supply and rate of entry into teaching, was seen as the the source of problem – without its creation of cheap, uncertificated teachers, the certificate would be worth more. The glut of cheap teachers was an economic threat to the NUT and a necessity for the Board. For a time, the struggle between the teachers and employers was represented by the fight for a Teachers Register aimed at control over entry, and therefore over supply and, thus, an improved standard of living.

The elementary teacher had been treated, under the Revised Code and later in poorly organised parts of the country, as a menial, a state servant working on in a centralised or cost-effective system. With the rising importance of the 'human capital' approach to education influencing the State, and the increased resistance and political power of the teachers, a new controlling force was required – more sophisticated than direct control. The notion of a Teachers Professional Register was of some value to the state, though they saw it differently to the teachers.

Initially, a Bill to propose the Teachers' Register excluded the elementary teachers because of the expected resistance of an Education Department with a very different view on controlling teachers:

> the relation in which such teachers stand to the Education Department forbids the interference of any other authority. Those who act as elementary teachers are trained so to act and are paid for

their services by the State. It is not unreasonable to expect that the paymaster, acting on behalf of the public, should insist on imposing his own conditions, and seeking precisely the qualifications which he may deem adequate for the fulfilment of these conditions.[6]

Eventually, a compromise was reached in that a professional Register was created in 1902 but was divided into two groups (Columns A and B) of certificated teachers and Secondary teachers, even though the enabling Act made no reference to such a division. The Board, and particularly, Morant, its Permanent Secretary, wished to divide the two groups of teachers on social as well as educational grounds. The teachers' resistance, and the growing feeling that Secondary teaching was about to be controlled by the State, led to a temporary alliance with the Secondary teachers. Yoxall, Secretary of the NUT, addressed the Headmaster's Conference on this theme:

I think you too believe that at the bottom of all this, at the top of all this, is the great struggle which impends in this country, which has indeed begun in this country, between the existence of teachers and teaching as a profession, a claim you rightly put forward and the demand for administrators in this country to reduce teaching to a State function and teachers to State functionaries.[7]

The argument for a Register which prevailed in the NUT was on the basis that the Teachers' Register would control entry into the profession. As circumstances changed during the period from 1910 to 1917 with the salaries campaign, and as it became obvious that the State did not intend to relinquish its power to a Registration Council, then the teachers considered other means of resisting the State's right to manage education. The strategy changed but the need remained the same.

We have discussed one example of the growing pressures on teachers by their employers, in London, and the way in which the National Union of Teachers sought by means of different policies to resist; to control the workplace. In this thumbnail sketch, injustice is done to the complexities of the issues involved but we want to show that an alternative perspective on teachers' behaviour and class consciousness is possible to sustain.

The financial pressures on local authorities increased, and then with the rise of inflation (between 1910 and 1913, retail prices rose by nine per cent), their need to economise, wherever possible, grew. They often substituted the cheaper uncertificated teachers for the certificated ones, sacked married women teachers and replaced them with single girls or they increased the responsibilities of the certificated teacher. In 1910, the NUT Tenure Committee suggested the local authorities were about to take desperate measures for they had heard:

a proposal was made that a large number of Authorities should combine to enforce a uniform *reduced* scale of salaries.[8]

By 1913, teacher resistance to the economies, the local

authority pressure and the increasing cost of living made the Tenure Committee again report that:

> there is in the teaching profession a widespread movement corresponding to the recent unrest in the industrial sphere. Attempts to economise at the expense of the teacher are giving place to agitations on the part of the teachers to secure more adequate salaries and better increments.[9]

The Union Executive had to act in response to the growing resistance of teachers, and it produced a recommended Union scale of salaries and a Special Salaries (or Action Committee) to help to organise local Association in dispute.

The teacher described by Helen Hamilton, in the *Compleat Schoolmarm* was changing:

> Despised, ill-paid and shunned
>   By those you serve so well
> Respectable but not respected.
>   Derided and mocked.
> You yet accept your fate
>   Unmurmuring, without reproach . . .
> Labourers everywhere may demand their full hire,
>   And perhaps even get it.
> But you have been taught
>   not to think about 'screws'
> So sordid to do it!
>   Oh wily, arch-wily employers.[10]

It was the teachers in the rural areas, often living on a bare subsistence level, isolated from each other and teaching in one- or two-teacher schools, who began to petition and send deputations to their local Authorities. The first big fight came in Herefordshire. Since 1904, the Union had been trying to raise local wages. The County had the lowest education rates in the country and was controlled, like most rural areas, by the farmers and the gentry. The local authority even had a standing minute that any discussion of salaries was out of order! Eventually the local Association used a tactic previously used in other Union disputes – mass resignations. From 1 January 1914, a hundred teachers resigned followed by a hundred and twenty nine others. National and local newspapers seem to have supported the teachers; the *Daily News* referred to 'sweated teachers' and the *Birmingham Post* recognised a new state of affairs:

> In the noise of industrial warfare, in the clamour over the wages of artisans, we are inclined to forget the humbler members of the professional classes. For them, too, the battle for existence is growing harder and harder. In many ways, it is time to say that they are far worse off than the men of the industrial unions. But so far they have not attempted combination.[11]

The Herefordshire Authority, like that of West Ham, tried to recruit Scottish teachers as 'blacklegs' and did not shirk from paying much more to the 'blackleg' teachers than they had to their own teachers. At the same time, they pleaded the impossibility of raising the rates to pay for the striker's pay demands. The Board of Education eventually wrote to Colonel Decie, who was in charge of the Authority's Salary Committee, expressing concern and suggesting that Exchequer grants, payable to local authorities for 'maintaining educational efficiency' might be withdrawn. This reminder by the State that education was still a bare necessity, if no more than that, helped to bring Herefordshire to a compromise with the Union but one in which the Union was recognised and a *scale* of salaries was agreed. This battle by the most oppressed of the Union's teachers galvanised the others throughout the country. The *Schoolmaster* gave full reports of the strike and later ran a 'Enthusiasts Column' on strikes, disputes and ways of recruiting new teachers.

When the Salary Campaign grew it depended on the initiative and militancy of the local Association. This was a positive advantage as a national strike would have broken a Union so divided in working conditions, areas and organisation. As the 1914 Annual Report said:

> ... the Local or County Association must be the unit of action if any good is to accrue, as a full knowledge of local circumstances and difficulties is the first condition of success. The time and method of action can only be best known to those who are in close touch with the district and with all the local conditions.[12]

Local actions might vary, from unsuccessful petitions to strikes. By 1915, half the three hundred and twenty one local education authorities in England and Wales, were in dispute. The greatest improvement to wages came in the rural areas, spurred by the Herefordshire action. The Union Executive called off the campaign, for patriotic reasons, when the World War began.

Some points that must be mentioned in relation to this campaign, between 1912 and 1914, are first, that it happened in a period of teacher shortage and the NUT actively discouraged young people from becoming teachers; the number of pupil teachers had fallen from eleven thousand in 1906–07 to one thousand five hundred in 1913–14. Second, local associations found natural allies in the labour movement. The *Schoolmaster* constantly referred to local public meetings addressed by teachers, unionists and labour councillors, and trades councils addressed by teachers. This was a natural development of the earlier calls for joint action for working class education. Third, there seems to have been a changed attitude by the Board of Education, responding to a policy for an improved education for an efficient Britain, which altered their attitude to Councils who held to an earlier policy of cheapness and minimal education. The Board produced documents *recommending* certain class sizes, and it was encouraging an independence or creative attitude by teachers to the curriculum. The Councils, especially in rural areas, represented an older tradition. The intervention of the State in educational provision, as well as many other fields of government, in the post 1900 period, changed its relationship with its indirect employees. (We regard local authorities – created in 1902 in England and Wales – as being part of the state but a policy of creating local buffers, or indirect agents, was not always effective for direct intervention in times of crisis by the centralized authorities. The degree of autonomy, especially in this period, allowed local authorities to act as semi-autonomous agents in some areas./ There were to be many discussions and minutes, about, for instance, the new status and control of, teachers – as civil servants etc. The Board never intervened at West Ham in 1907 but it did at Herefordshire in 1914 – why?

The rapid rise in retail prices in the war period, up by forty per cent between 1914 and 1916, led to many workers fighting for war 'bonuses'. The NUT *had* to restart its salary campaign in 1916 because of the cost of living and a revitalised militancy. The situation was exacterbated by the deteriorating conditions in schools as many of the trained teachers had joined the Army. A steady 'dilution' of work conditions and employment was advocated and practised by local authorities allowing untrained adults, disabled soldiers or middle class women, to take classes. Tropp says:

> Many of the schools and training colleges were taken over for use as billets for the troops, hospitals ... the strictly 'educational' work of the schools suffered from the amount of time devoted to war savings, school gardens and allotments, the col-collection of wild fruits and horse chestnuts.[13]

The President of the NUT, C.W. Crook, an eminent Conservative, remarked in his Presidential address that the London Education Committee:

in its absurd panic at the outbreak of war is recalling teachers and children in the middle of the summer holiday, its sweating of supply teachers and its serious reduction of staff under the specious plea of redistribution have seriously impaired the efficiency of the schools.[14]

The restarting of the salaries campaign during the war, from 1916 onwards, accelerated the movement of many local associations teachers towards the labour movement and the Labour Party. There always had been, in the *Schoolmaster*, mention of teachers or local NUT associations being involved with Trades Councils (or, more accurately, Trades and Labour Councils) – for instance, in Swansea, Ebbw Vale, Nottingham, Bradford and Burton on Trent. The TUC Conference at Swansea in 1901 was welcomed officially by the Secretary of the Reception Committee who was a teacher and member of the NUT; he began by saying that the NUT should be affiliated to the TUC, and then demanded that there should be:

a general uprising of workers in protest against the attempts made to rob the children of toilers of facilities for higher education.[15]

Individual teachers joined the Independent Labour Party or the Social Democratic Federation, and later the Plebs League. They were elected to Trades Councils (a Class Teacher's delegate was President of the Northampton Trades Council in 1917) and in at least one instance, the NUT Association was the founder organisation of the

Labour Party (in Pembroke where the NUT President became the President of the new Labour Party). Sometimes teachers became the organisers of, or assisted in, other Unions, like the Agricultural Workers Union. Many leading socialists in this period were teachers, like John Maclean and James Maxton, and other recruits to socialism later became Presidents of the NUT, like W.G. Cove and Leach Manning.

The impetus towards the Labour movement was twofold – Labour was the party of education and it was the party of the working class. In both these ways, it attracted teacher support. A recognition of a shared class interest seems to have been a strong feature of this period (the Salary Campaign and after) – teachers felt themselves to be working class and the labour movement tried hard to encourage this feeling. When the Rhondda Class Teachers' Association joined the local Trades and Labour Council in March 1913, the *Rhondda Socialist* editorialised that:

> a new era is about to dawn for the class teachers of the Rhondda, they have finally recognised the fact that they are workers – some of them slaves on the brink of poverty, others actually in poverty on the brink of destitution and subject to petty tyranny from those in authority over them.[16]

A great push towards Labour was given by teachers outside the NUT. A small union called the National Union of Uncertificated Teachers affiliated to the TUC in 1919, and was consistently supported in debate by unions like the Building Trades Workers.

After the massive Bradford Charter in 1916, where Labour produced a clear call for progress in education, the ties between many teachers and the Labour movement and Party drew closer together. The Labour Party was seen as *the* party of education. This trend in the NUT took a positive turn in January 1917. Birmingham teachers had called a meeting on the salary campaign, after the Union Executive was unwilling to do so, to which representatives of 250 local Associations came. This conference made clear proposals for new, vigorous action in the campaign, calling for a strengthened sustentation or strike fund and affiliation to the local and national labour movement. Discussion of these issues dominated the *Schoolmaster* throughout 1917 and early 1918, and was followed closely in the Labour and Tory Press. Under pressure from members, including some of the Executive, the Executive created a special Committee to look at the issue of Labour Party affiliation, though it was also mandated to consider the options of Civil service status and self-governing professionalism. The whole referendum on these issues was very unclear to many teachers; for instance, unlike Labour Party affiliation, it was not clear if the other two options were strong possibilities or wishful thinking. Indeed, a leading proposer of affiliation refused to discuss it as an *alternative* to self-governing industrial trades unionism, as we shall see later, was adopted by many socialists in the Union as a combination of self-government and class consciousness, and the term 'professionalism' could be used by them to express this idea.

Crook, a leading member of the NUT Executive and a

member of the Conservative Party, did not use 'professionalism' in this way, nor did the *Times* in its constant leaders counselling teachers on avoiding the path of militant unionism and class unity. Crook's position on affiliation (which, in fact, is very like Troop's later position in his book) was that the Unions had:

> succeeded by aloofness ... from all parties and have obtained our improvements by the strength of our case, and not by throwing the whole of our weights into any one political circus.[18]

He also argued that affiliation would cause parental difficulties on the issue of teacher neutrality. Writers like Crook, who discussed professionalism as a calling above politics, were generally Conservatives, though one of the proposers for affiliation was described as a 'life-long Conservative'. There was a mass defection of Conservative teachers to the Labour Party in this period, culminating in a plea to Baldwin in 1923 (by Crook among others) to produce an education policy quickly to stem the flow.

Labour affiliation supporters, in their meetings up and down the country, generally argued that the interests of capital and labour were not identical, workers were exploited (teachers being workers) and that teachers taught the working class children. Corlett, a teacher, wrote to the *Schoolmaster* in 1917:

> we suggest affiliation with the Labour Party because we believe that if we are to live we must act as a body, and only by combined political action can we obtain economic freedom.[19]

Alderman Conway, a teacher from Bradford, illustrates the confusing, even irrelevant, nature of the referendum by arguing on the one hand that:

> in Bradford, there were 40,000 organised workers behind the teachers when they made a move and they were getting today the largest bonus in the country.[20]

and on the other hand, he held the view that affiliation should be left for the distant future after local Associations had been encouraged to join the Trades Councils, and the Union had joined the TUC.

As it was, the new Labour Party constitution, creating a national organisation rather than a federation and encouraging individual membership and appealing to 'producers by hand or brain' (agreed in 1918) made the whole affiliation issue rather irrelevant, and Crook suggested that this was likely to affect the Referendum result.

The *Daily Herald*, which gave full support to teachers in the Salary Campaign and published regular reports on local disputes and settlements, trades council affiliation and the 'equal pay for equal work' campaign, virtually ignored the Referendum. This seems a much more *practical* response to an issue which seemed to be diverting the teachers from other struggles. It described teachers, in an article on the NUT Conference in 1919, as:

> conservative in outlook, painfully respectable and ultra-respectful in method. Nowadays, however, many of the teachers are actively associated with

the Labour Party and are determined eventually
to secure the affiliation of their Union to the Party
which they regard as the only means of attaining
solidarity amongst all who work, whether with
head or hand, or both. They have taken a lesson
from their new associates, strikes have come,
having regard to their inadequate salaries and the
puny war bonuses, it is not surprising. Teachers
have achieved a considerable amount of success
in consequence . . . [21]

The Times, on the other hand, covered the Union
debate on Affiliation, assisted by a regular column,
National Union Notes, written mainly by Crook. The
editorials in *The Times* created a systematic policy on
the teachers, which was very similar to the arguments
used by Fisher in his Education Bill meetings. Status and
remuneration could now be achieved by the Teachers
Registration Council, which might even, though the
Union had been useful in the past, supersede the Union.

the future of England is in a very real sense at
last in the hands of teachers . . . Will they sacrifice
to sectional interests, to religious difficulties, to
class prejudices, the greatest opportunity that has
ever been offered to a profession.[22]

The old education system did exploit teachers and did
ignore the real education of the working class but, it
was explained, this was all changing. Fisher, for instance,
made it very clear that the State required new, skilled

workmen for the new scientific industries, the production
of good citizens and 'harmonious relations between
capital and labour'. A new deal for teachers in this new
education was to be created. Teachers had to be saved
from the dangerous path they were treading; that of
organisation, class alliances and action. When Ramsay
MacDonald, in a Parliamentary debate on the new Bill,
referred to the 'psychological' steps needed to improve
education, and that the elementary schoolteacher needed
work which would be 'interesting, dignified and invested
with a certain amount of glory', it is clear that the State
could mean something other than the militant teachers
by 'professionalism', and that 'teachers self-government'
was a psychological step. The creation of the myth of
partnership and autonomy can be traced to the needs of
a State and its tactics in controlling teachers. Fisher,
referring to the 'noble, dignified teaching profession', also
began to raise the question of teachers, the new guardians
of the 'human capital' of tomorrow, to be part of a new,
national service:

> I regard the establishment on a sound basis, of an
> efficient and devoted corps of teachers as a public
> necessity, less obvious perhaps, but no less im-
> perative than the maintenance of the fighting
> forces of the Crown.[23]

The State was now to be seen as the friend of the teacher,
a referee or ombudsman. It had shown increasing interest in remuneration and status of teachers, and was
now guaranteeing a minimum salary and superannuation.

He asked the teachers not to 'condemn the system' because *some* local authorities might not have carried out their responsibilities. It soon became clear that, in return for these guarantees by the State, it wished to create a new 'professionalism' or management ideology. Fisher expected a:

> measure of unstinted and zealous service on behalf of the childhood of the country.[24]

What was to be the position of the Union? Fisher continued:

> ... the NUT has played a most valuable part in watching over the material interests of the profession. . . . But as the State takes a more and more direct interest in the material conditions of the profession, and as these material conditions become more and more improved, then I hope that the activities of the NUT, which is such a powerful instrument for influencing opinion in this country, may be more and more concentrated upon what I may call the *spiritual* and intellectual interests of the teachers' work.[25]

The Times soon began to call for a 'true' professional spirit.

The discontent amongst the teachers, clearly to be seen in the education and national Press, and in the news and correspondence columns of the *Schoolmaster*, was not new. What was new was the pace and size of the discontent – weekly meetings calling for radical policies – and the determination to act. William Howard, in an article in the *Socialist Review* called 'The unrest amongst teachers', discussed their new militancy:

> In some parts of the country they have even consummated that painful process [becoming bolder] and gone on strike. This in itself is a tremendous advance, for up to a few years ago to mention the word strike was enough to give the average teacher an apoplectic seizure ... while [strikes] do not show that teachers, as a whole, have learned the lesson of mass movement, they are indicative of a change of outlook, a new spirit which will spread until it compels a complete revolution in the conditions under which teachers labour.[26]

Goldstone, a Labour M.P. and NUT Executive member, in *The Times*, remarked on this massive discontent:

> It is a mistake to assume, however, as some critics do, that there is a constant stimulus from the officers and officials of the Union to persistent, and on occasion, drastic action. The present discontent is widespread and is essentially a rank and file development, which as a matter of fact, is very difficult to find sufficient representatives to direct.[27]

The strike in Rhondda epitomises the struggles of the teachers in this period – they were young, male and female, certificated and uncertificated, they worked together and they were strongly influenced by the labour movement and its ideas. More than this, the Rhondda strike won the national award for the teachers – it was such a resounding victory that its reverberations shook the Union. Rhondda was an exceptional struggle but it represented the new direction of the Union.

As has been noted, the Rhondda teachers had joined the Trades and Labour Council in 1913 – a Council dominated by the miners. This was the period when Syndicalist ideas were growing strongly in the South Wales Miners Federation and were reviving and creating an industrial strength and radical evangelism which was confirmed by the success of the Cambrian Combine strike in 1918. The Plebs League, the movement for an Independent Working Class Education, based on Marxism and strongly influenced by the new Industrial Trades Unionism was active in the valleys, and two of the teachers' strike leaders were tutors in the League, W.G. Cove and Gwen Ray. The younger, Syndicalist miners were strong supporters of the teachers; though older labour leaders did not see teachers as part of the working class, they themselves were losing control of the union to the younger militants. The teachers were, in turn, affected by their ideas on union organisation and strength. When the Class Teacher's Association called the strike, it did so for the certificated *and* the uncertificated teachers, even though the latter were ineligible for membership of the NUT or for strike pay. No divisions, based on the old craft union ideas, for them – instead the power of united action by all those concerned in the industry. Strong support was given to the teachers by the Trades and Labour Council, Labour Councillors (like A.J. Cook, the future miners' leader) and the miners' lodges. Cove had previously been threatened with dismissal because of his union work and a deputation, including miners and railwaymen, went to the Council. A miners' delegate said that they:

> asked to be acquainted with the decision of the Council so that they might convey the result to their lodges. He answered them that the matter would not be allowed to rest.[28]

Only after twelve hundred teachers went on strike in February 1919 did the NUT support them with a strike office and by sending an Executive member down.

The teachers of the Rhondda appealed for support from the people – not on the old grounds of the NUT, that of the quality and provision of working class education, nor on the grounds expressed in the Referendum, that of Labour uniting them as the party of education and progress – but they appealed as socialists. Teachers were economically oppressed, like the miners; they were 'skilled workmen' fighting for 'trade union principles' and 'downing tools'; they were 'sweated labour' and 'wage slaves'. They acknowledged their lack of trade union experience and their past attempts to pretend that economic laws did not apply to them. They attacked the old Labour representatives on the council. This was not an appeal by the timid. The teachers were *demanding* support with the confidence of fellow workers and socialists.

95

The strength of the attack shook the Government who used the new possibilities for increased rate support still being discussed in Parliament to try and solve the strike. After the teachers returned reluctantly to work, they were awarded, in April, a wage scale which doubled the wages of most teachers. For the first time the union scale of salaries had been achieved without compromise. W.G. Cove, whose reputation in the union soon led him to the position of Union President (in 1922), wrote in the Rhondda Leader, during the strike, a sophisticated plea for the new unionism:

> One of the factors determining the market price of labour is the power of the trades unions. Trades unions tend to force up the market price. Relatively speaking, the teachers' unions have been weak. We are now in the Rhondda experiencing a revival of unionism amongst the teachers, which is expressing itself in an effort to raise the market price, and the trade unionist who opposes us is endeavouring to thwart the inevitable expression of a reunified unionism. The market price of a commodity – of the commodity called labour – is the standard of the capitalist employer and no sound trade unionist can use the standard of the capitalist employer.[29]

The example of the Rhondda teachers, in working together with the uncertificated teachers, changed the policy of the Union. The NUT had always feared that their economic gains and their work conditions would be eroded by the uncertificated teachers, admitted by the State, and this had returned in the war; Crook remarked upon the intentions of local authorities retaining un-trained, emergency workers, supposedly a 'war freedom' only. But instead of strengthening their craft elitism, the NUT followed the lead of the Rhondda and admitted uncertificated teachers to membership. The strength of the industrial union idea and its influence in the union came from the victory of the Rhondda teachers.

The 1919 Cheltenham Conference was a radical con-ference. It was led from the floor and the Executive had to constantly explain and examine its proposals. As Goldstone commented:

> the districts in which industrial activity in trade unions circles is greatest, produce the teachers who are the strongest advocates of a 'forward policy' in the NUT.[30]

What happened between 1910 and 1920 is significant for teachers today. The social and political structure of the society they were in was breaking down. Working class consciousness and actions were forcing the employers on to the defensive. The operation of the state was under attack.

It is of interest to read the discussions of the teachers at the time and to see how the rapidly changing nature of the society was reflected in their thoughts and actions. The nature of the questions asked about their purpose and value and what they should do are vital to an under-standing of their position today. Teachers, like other kinds of newly-organized sections of the working class, suffered from a kind of amnesia which, by the 1930s had almost eliminated collective thought about the pre-1920 period.

The relationship between the teachers and the state altered in the post-1920 period. Direct controls were removed and 'indirect rule', following the practice of our colonial administration, was substituted. The restructuring of society, with a prominent role for the state, did not necessarily mean direct control: for instance, with the rise of intelligence testing and examinations in the school syllabus came the reduction of Board of Education direct control over teachers and their curriculum.

The struggle over the role of education under capitalism and the place of teachers within it, exemplified by the teachers' actions in the period 1910 and 1920, has surely many direct parallels with today.

Unions, Employers and the State

The history of white collar workers (clerks, civil servants or local authority administrative staff) bears a close resemblance to the development of teacher unionism, yet references made to the parallel nature of their struggles and problems are few in histories of either branch of the working class. Indeed teachers' problems and concerns are usually only expressed within the context of the development of the education system, with its own Acts, regulations and significant events.

It has already been noted that teachers found it difficult to organise in many areas where they were isolated from each other or worked within small schools. This was also the case in many schools outside the urban areas at the turn of the century. The urban teachers were better organised and it was they who led the fight for better pay and conditions of work. Their direct employers, the Local Authorities, were also under direct pressure from the increase in the urban population and the consequent demand for services. The low rateable value of many areas and the 'squeeze' on the Government rate support grant in the early years of this century, the rapid inflation rate and the decline in the quality of work accentuated by the war, produced a radical shift in the attitudes and actions of the teachers. In turn, the reaction of a central government and its allies to this change produced a new policy towards teachers which, while not different in its overall aim (of control), used very different methods and tactics. The period from 1917 to 1921 marked the height of the teacher militancy. Subsequent attacks by the Government (in the Geddes Committee proposals) and the local authorities severely damaged the gains of the post-war period and isolated teachers from the labour movement, if not its political wing, the Labour Party.

Our discussion of the teacher's concern for the quality of their work and their responsibilities has been brief. We have suggested that 'professionalism' as such is a complex area. In the historical period studied, at least three versions of it can be seen: within teachers discussions both Left and Right use the term 'professionalism' in very different ways – one as a recognition of separate identity and responsibility, the other as a form of syndicalism; the Government also begin to propose a 'professionalism' shorn of its unionism and stressing responsibility and status.

Throughout our analysis of these events and ideas, it seems clear to us that teachers were concerned with employment and employers – whether local or national. Their problems, although sometimes couched in 'educational' terms, seem very like the problems of all wage-earners. Our intention now is to look at employees of local, national or private institutions to see in what ways similarities and parallels may be drawn.

At the beginning of the century, many white collar workers were in receipt of larger incomes than manual workers but the process of reducing, or narrowing, this differential was in motion. White collar workers were growing in number. The small offices and accounting rooms were changing. Larger concentrations of white collar staff, their specialisation into different facets of clerical or other work, and their assignment to grades all affected their elite, priviledged position at work.

Clerks in the late Victorian period were gradually losing their advantages of pay and conditions of work over manual workers. The rise of a state education system was reducing the value of their own education and allowing the working class or elementary school pupil to take jobs as boy clerks and women clerks. The rise in scale of the offices meant that promotion was slow and increasingly a matter of grades. By the 1880s clerks were de-skilled and unable to restrict entry into their field by 'craft' control. There was fierce competition for jobs and wages were low. *The Daily Post*, in 1877, pointed out this de-skilling process:

> The intellectual work of the clerk is far less worthy
> of that name than is generally supposed. ... In
> fact, the higher class of mechanics, pattern-
> makers, smiths, engineers and printers expend as
> much pure intellectual effort.[31]

The fairly close, if paternal, relationship between the
clerk and his employer was breaking down due to the
larger offices, increasing specialization of some tasks and
the routinization of others. This situation is common to
all kinds of work but occurred later in the white collar
field. De-personalization of work, where the job not the
job holder is important, also meant that control over work
tended to be, not personal, but by the application of
formal, bureaucratic procedures and rules.

The response of the clerks – and of civil servants,
teachers and local authority administrative officers faced
with a similar decline of work conditions and pay and a
routinisation of work – was in association. These associations had one thing, at least, in common – they preferred
to distinguish themselves from trade unions which, at that
time, were mainly composed of manual workers. The
National Association of Local Government Officers, at
its inauguration in 1905, was described as 'concerned with
the independent status, and to further the interests, of
the local government officer. His task was to assist the
local councils and community'.[32] This concern for its
public or community duty is a common strand in most
white collar public service work, although it varies in
ideological strength, from period to period, from section
to section.

NALGO has a union (or association) history which is very similar to the NUT. Its protestation about its 'association' status rather than 'union' status is echoed by the founding declaration of the NUT but its consequent attempt to recruit members by this talk of 'duty' does not seem so successful as their recruitment on the basis of class or personal interest. For instance, when East Ham Council in 1908 (note the parallel with the NUT's dispute with West Ham in 1907) sought to save £2,000 by dismissing twenty two officers (including the deputy town clerk), abolishing overtime payment and increasing working hours, NALGO officers were very keen to fight the proposals because of their concern that lack of action might be seen as weakness by members who might, in turn, leave for the National Union of Clerks.[33] Tactics used in this period included letters and petitions to the Councillors and, later, the Press. This moderate policy must have encouraged councils like Newcastle-upon-Tyne, Cleethorpes, Congleton and Walsall in their disputes with NALGO; the last three councils demanded that all applications for salary increases be accompanied by letters of resignation! In its weakness, NALGO looked for strong allies. In 1912, it tried to establish a joint headquarters with the NUT (called 'Municipal House'), which failed. In 1917, its journal suggested a tripple alliance with the NUT and the National Poor Law Officer's Association, which failed due to the 'collective bargaining success of the NUT'.[34] By 1918, the issues and ideas that affected the NUT were shaking NALGO – in the Annual Conference at Blackpool, the General Secretary, referring to the Labour

Party affiliation debate, said:

> the tendency (of affiliation with the labour move-
> ment) is growing, our Association cannot ignore
> it.[35]

By the 1919 Conference, the industrial and social
turmoil affecting most workers was in evidence during a
debate, on immediate registration to the TUC, proposed
by a branch in South Wales. What worried some NALGO
members, as expressed by the Executive, was the lack
of sympathy for the professional worker by the general
unions. Judging by their debate, there was a mutual
distrust similar to the one the NUT tried to overcome – at
least, in branches like the Rhondda. So many members of
NALGO, or ex-service members, were joining other
Unions noted for their militancy; Spoor called this a
'flood' after the 1919 Conference.[36] In January, 1920 a
NALGO Special Conference was held because of this
crisis in the 'professional' association. Many of the branch
delegates had mandates to resign from NALGO if it was
not reconstituted as a 'trade union'. The next conference
in June resolved this issue when a majority of three to
one voted in favour of becoming a 'recognised' trade
union. An organising Secretary was created and a target
of fifty thousand members set.

Aspects of the term 'professionalism' were used in
NALGO as they were in the NUT. It was a recognition of
their social and economic differences from the manual
working class organised into trade unions. It was also a
way of escaping a recognition of their role; they substituted a value of public service for the difficult task of

ascertaining their labour-value. This constant feature of the ideology of these two white collar unions' was stronger in their early years but the necessity for their employers to reduce this level of disinterested service in their expansion, routinisation and control eventually led to its partial recreation as an argument for differentiation and separation from the working class and, later, as a defence of standards of public service in a time of 'cuts'.

A concept of 'justice' was often used in NALGO, NUT and other white collar discussions of their employment and pay problems. It is not class war which is being discussed, nor the recognition that injustice is a necessary part of the system, but almost a belief in the 'good case', 'poor' argument and 'antagonistic' individuals involved in their pay and work. This came to mean that in the pre-war years it was, in NALGO and the NUT's case, the local authority that was the problem and a national pay scale that could be the solution. Most of the white collar unions – the Bank Clerks, NALGO, the Civil Service Associations – were demanding regular machinery to deal with matters of wages and conditions in their field as a whole. At the same time, the war-time government (and the later post-war government) had created the original Whitley Committee in direct response to the growing unrest amongst the working class; its brief was to secure a 'permanent improvement in the relations between employers and workmen'.[37] While these Whitley Committees were generally unwelcome in the strongly organised industries, weaker white collar unions tended to see them as advantageous. Certainly for most NUT members, the Burnham scales initially agreed were better than their existing salaries though, in fact, the aware only kept up with the rapid rise of inflation from the pre-war period. The General Secretary of the Civil Service Clerical Associations believed that the creation of a 'staff' side under the Whitley system helped to speed up the unity of a Civil Service divided by many 'grade' associations and range of salaries. The NALGO executive was, bluntly, intoxicated by the National Whitley Council. Spoor details the advantages as: first, NALGO would become the sole negotiator because it was the biggest staff organisation; second, a national employers organisation had to be created, for the first time, to deal with pay and conditions; and third, in an interesting comment, it was suggested that branch autonomy would dwindle with national negotiations, and 'skilled professional negotiators' would replace them.[38] The weakness of NALGO (as of the NUT in many areas) led to this welcoming of Whitley; for instance, in 1931, 1,200 out of 1,700 local Councils did not have salary scales (they fixed their own wages) or a grievance structure.

It is a feature of the period, remarked upon by commentators, that the union militancy displayed by the white collar workers[39] had to be defeated by the Government or employers. This was not easy prior to 1921 as the unions were recruiting strongly in a period of industrial expansion.[40] With the post-war slump from the early Twenties, the new union membership declined rapidly; for instance, the Clerks Union membership fell from 47,528 in 1920 to 7,442 in 1924 (less than its 1913 membership).[41]

A further reason why a white collar defeat was necessary

was the increasing alliance with the political wing of the Labour movement, the Labour Party.[42] The Civil Service Clerical Association combined an aggressive recruitment policy with a Labour Party alliance. NALGO found it was losing members in areas where Labour Councils only employed trade union labour. As we saw with the teachers referendum on Labour Party affiliation, this move to the Labour Party had many reasons behind it; self-interest, a new Utopia, a working class alliance or alliance with a powerful ally. In all these manifestations, it was regarded as a danger by many employers.

The counter-attack by the employers took many forms but its goal seems clear. It was to isolate the white collar unions from their membership and from their Labour movement connections, to reduce them to insignificance and then to propose alternative policies for their white collar workers.

In a period of labour shortage, rising inflation and attacks on working conditions, the unions were increasingly strong and determined, influenced by grassroots membership and other union actions. White collar unions, weak in organisation and traditions, turned to a positive policy of actions built around strong local membership bases. The NUT pushed its claim forward by supporting local associations, who were willing and organised to fight their local authorities, and used their successes to galvanise other associations or influence other employers. Elvin, the Clerk's Union Secretary, described this process as:

a guerilla campaign ... [which] resulted in a

gradual general recognition, first by individual firms, then District Associations, and lastly, by their National Body.[43]

According to Bain, white collar unions generally followed this means of struggle for pay and recognition in the immediate post-war period. The employers eventually felt, and they certainly did after 1919 in education, that a national basis for negotiation was necessary. This is where the Government's creation of the original Whitley Committee can be seen as a recognition that the State could 'referee' on a fair, national basis the relations between employers and employees and that it was advantageous to do so when employees were organising and discussing radical political alliances and solutions. But we have also seen that the white collar unions saw advantages in Whitley Committees as well; the rank and file pressure would be controlled, the industrial conditions of employment would be equalised and a reasoned, just case could be presented by skilled negotiations.

The employers used sophisticated tactics involving pay awards less than the cost of living but given without struggle, creating disunity; for many urban teachers, the Burnham award was not only less than the inflation in the period covered but *less than their local struggles had produced.* This period also saw the beginning of grading exercises covering many white collar workers; bank clerks were now placed on grades ranging from 'office machine minder to certificated bankers'.[44] The Civil Service already had a grading system which was recognised in 1920 with greater standardisation. Office workers were graded, from routine jobs and semi-skilled work right up to Office Manager. Workers were isolated from each other and from different grades.

Where a union was weak, and this was the case with most of the new white collar unions, even the temporary benefits gained from the Whitley Committees could be withdrawn. NALGO submitted an identical claim to the recently approved Whitley claim for the civil servants. This was eventually agreed by the Council in May 1920, yet the Councils (Urban, County and Rural District) Associations refused to implement the agreement. The Government, using the argument that compulsion on the defaulting authorities was impossible due to the voluntary nature of the Whitley Committees, refused to intervene and the Committee collapsed in early 1921. This was followed by three years of local Council attacks.[45] Almost exactly the same situation occurred for the NUT in the Burnham negotiations. Several local councils refused to implement the new scales and the NUT was involved in long strikes at Lowestoft and Gateshead when the Government refused to intervene. Anyway, in 1923, the Geddes economy proposals reduced the teacher's wage unilaterally. The stable alliance between the Civil Service Clerical Association and the TUC and Labour Party, resulting in firm support during the 1926 General Strike, led the Government (by the Trade Union Act of 1927) to make it illegal for civil servants to affiliate to outside political or industrial organisations.

Another tactic of the employers and State included the formation of staff associations or the recognition of 'professional' associations. For instance, in 1923, the

House of Commons passed a resolution:

> That local authorities, banks, insurance and ship-
> ping companies and other employers of profes-
> sional and clerical workers should follow the
> example of the Government in recognising the
> organisation of these workers.[46]

Along with recognition came a sponsored view of white
collar workers in local and national administration, or
services like education, as being 'professionals' – defined
as the unselfish service of the public which could not allow
an alliance with sectional or class interests. The teachers
received a full broadside of this view in *The Times* editorials
and in the speeches of Fisher. It was made clear that the
days of penny-pinching and lack of recognition for their
public service were at an end, and passing reference was
made to the role of the NUT in helping that period to
pass. Yet the acceptance of new salary scales involved a
new relationship and responsibility. Unions would become unnecessary or too crude to deal with the higher
demands of public service and educational ideals demanded of them. This appeal must have had attractions
for the teachers on the sidelines of the events that had
happened; teachers untouched by action or the new
arguments of class solidarity and consciousness. It appealed also to the new Labour technocrats, believing in
the coming rationally organised Utopia with its recognition of service and intellectual skills, propagandized by
the Webbs. It would appear as the final recognition of
the struggles for education against reactionary councils,

squires and employers, and their just reward.

When the employer's counter-attack came these 'professional' appeals looked a bit thin but by that time the social climate had altered. Even the industrial working class was in retreat. Klingender, explaining the rapid decline of the Clerks Union, describes the difficulty of opposing this appeal by the State, easpecially among the unorganised clerks:

> the task of approaching them in the numerous small offices, especially in the City was as difficult as ever ... it was not easy to convince the great mass of the clerks of the danger involved for their future position if they accepted present concessions as a bargain for the involvement of a permanent organisation.[47]

If the need for a

> strong unified clerical trade union ... preparing for the inevitable counter-offensive.[48]

had been recognised by more than a minority, Klingender believes the decline could have been halted. It must have been a similar problem for NALGO, faced with an uneven consciousness and organisation among its members, and the employer counter attack. The guerilla struggles needed a period of reorganisation and renewal that never came, and a leadership that did not see greater virtue in believing the state. The teachers were far better organised in a mass union, the NUT, but this period saw a separation of the militant members from the general membership – in the Twenties they moved into the Labour Party as councillors or, later, M.P.s, or into the Teacher's Labour League or the, later, National Association of Labour Teachers. They developed their ideas, conceived in the War and post-war years but curiously isolated in the Twenties and Thirties from the mass of teachers. Klingender found that the most militant clerks were often drawn away into the clerical sections of industrial unions leaving the bulk of the clerks without leadership except that given by their employers.

A further difficulty, noticed in the Rhondda by the local teachers, was the distrust of the white collar workers by the manual/skilled working class. This was also mentioned by Spoor in his history of NALGO – the concerns of the 'professional' worker seems to be given short shrift by the general unions. These concerns, according to Spoor, must be the antagonism to trade union sympathy strikes (in the early period), the alienation of support offered by Government Departments to their work, and a consequent feeling by other workers that 'public duty or service' and a consequent belief in the 'fairness' or neutrality of the State was misguided, to say the least. An article in *Plebs* in early 1916 discusses the difficulties between clerks and the working class[49] and is worth quoting from. The MFGB (The Miners Federation) had, at their 1911 Conference, declared for Industrial Unionism without ambiguity except

> the only workmen who are not included are the colliery office clerks, who are treated as the confidants of the employing class.

Teachers, Professionalism and Class

The writer of the article, a member of the Clerk's Union, reserved this attitude towards his 'fellow craftsmen'. Just like the arguments in *The Rhondda Socialist*, the writer distinguishes between their actions and their fundamental class position. Clerks do 'blackleg' and they may be 'confidants of the employing class', but they are a strong and growing section in industry and they need organising. More, the writer denies that:

> Clerks [are] *members* of the *employing* class. . . . The class dividing line of society, as I understand it, occurs precisely where the sale of labour power ends and exploitation begins, and I have yet to learn that clerks *qua* clerks possess any other than a commodity status as compared to manual workers . . .
>
> What of the clerk's wages, hours of employment and general office conditions? Are these very much different, in *effect* from those appertaining to manual employment?

He goes on to describe the low wages of the clerks and their unpaid overtime, and that, just like manual workers, enslavement or working class organisation is the only way.

There can be no denying the differences between the white collar and the manual workers, but those differences were being removed all the time. Distrust of each other was fostered by the employer, though there were *different* emphases placed by the two groups on struggle and tactics. These, too, were breaking down – the white collar was, it seems, seeking alliance with the labour movement because it was moving along the same historical path they had taken earlier – withdrawal of labour, recognition of class interests and class consciousness and irreconcilable interests with the employing class. Yet, the incomplete or unequal development amongst the white collar workers at this time led to its defeat, to schisms and to a renewed attempt by the employers to instil a policy of separate ideological development, built around the white collar concern for community service or the emphasis on merit, promotion and status, depending upon the location in the public or private sector.

Summary – Teachers and White Collar Workers

We have taken a short interlude from the teachers' history and a brief synopsis of white collar unionism because they illustrate a complexity about white collar/education work which can't simply be brushed aside by reference to managerial professional ideologies, status or contradictory class location. We shift from the review of theoretical analyses to examination of the problems that teachers and white collar workers actually faced and their ways of dealing with them.

For teachers, the period from 1912 to 1920 seems a watershed in their growing class consciousness and their relationship to the State. Recognising the difficulty of joining with members of a class which was partially hostile to the new white collar workers, they, nevertheless, recognised their allies and their class position. The resistance against unionisation which existed in many, small, paternal offices and schools was broken down by the development of large urban concentrations of white collar workers, their gradual sharing of ideas with militant workers and the way in which they were treated by their employers. Teachers and white collar workers did not just drift to the labour movement, their conditions of work and decline in pay rates forced them into a recognition of class interest.

For teachers, the problem of their work lay with their employer. In rural areas, the social and political domination of the Church was matched by the economic domination of the rich farmers; teachers were at their mercy in terms of their duties, pay and personal behaviour. In the cities, the urban teacher associations were often at odds with the economic and productivity policies of their employers, the School Boards or local authorities. The issues and responses of the teachers to their problems of employment varied from year to year but a clear development can be shown to 1921, as it can with white collar workers. Teachers in weak unionization (that is in rural areas or in the early years of the union) resisted the employers by petitions, letters, deputations, 'blacklisting' authorities or using the union solicitor. Teachers in strong unionized areas used these tactics but also openly threatened and protested; in the days of the School Boards, teachers joined with progressive education forces to take over reactionary School Boards at election times. As a whole the union began to recommend or support more direct action by their local associations, culminating in the salary campaign. The strikes and disputes grew in number, frequency and length as the conditions which created them also generated employer resistance to them.

The different policies of the union with regard to their employers can be found within a continuous concern to resist management. At different historical periods or in different geographical areas, this antagonism may give rise to different policies of the union but management resistance is always contained within these policies. The search for a self-governing profession was brought about because the state constantly undermined 'craft' skills and pay rates by allowing entry into the education system of uncertificated teachers or completely untrained supplementary teachers. A self-governing profession would have controlled the means of entry into teaching and halted the dilution of skill and lowering of remuneration. However, although this idea never completely died, the policy of the Union in the period studied here, moved away from self-governing professionalism to union action (resistance by strikes etc.) and by altering the recruitment policy of the union – towards an industrial unionism that would recruit all workers in education.

The move to the labour movement may have had several motives. For both the teachers and the white collar workers in government service there must have been a recognition of the public service element of labour policy. In the period studied, teachers did not see evidence of any Tory education policy for the mass of the nation's children apart from cost-cutting, or *laissez-faire*. Only Labour discussed the educational future of working class children and produced future policy statements. An element of the Labour Party at the time, based around the Webbs, propagandized for a state acting on behalf

115

of the community, not taken over by a class. This element of duty and service in a recognised, progressive state would not be openly antagonistic to many of the teacher's or local government officer's ideas. Labour was also attractive because of its strength – white collar workers, often isolated in small groups at their place of work felt they needed strong allies. Labour was growing, as were the white collar unions. As the local authorities and employers proved impervious to the usual tactics of petitions etc., then the policies and numbers of organised Labour appeared as the only possible support. The influence of the syndicalists, socialists and Marxists, although few in number, was felt by all workers, including white collar workers. Their arguments against the Lib-Lab Union leadership and Utopian socialism and for industrial unionism in support of the exploited workers affected the teachers in the Rhondda and in the debates on Labour affiliation and union tactics around the country. Their arguments broke down the isolation of teachers, created by their past actions and distrust of manual trades unionism. These new ideas held the possibility of class unity; both sides tried to convert each other.

Professionalism was an idea used by teachers. It could mean a public service or it could mean industrial control. It could mean not striking or joining Labour or it could mean defending working class education against employers. To some of the correspondents to *The Schoolmaster* in this period it meant a combination of these ideas – not striking *but* joining Labour; industrial control but not the Labour Party; a self-governing profession given by the state or achieved by resisting the local agents of the state but accepting the guarantees of the national state. If, by professionalism, we mean a concern for the quality of education, the resources of education and access to it by the working class, then this was probably the general view of the elementary schoolteachers, expressed in a number of (possibly contradictory) policies. What all, or most, of these policies had in common was a distrust of the managers or employers of the education system. At this period, the local state had only recently been created and the central state pursued a policy of delegation or informal control, acting as a benevolent neutral guardian of local affairs. The far-sighted policy of reducing conflict to local battles and solutions to national meetings seems to have been very successful in this period. The proposals of Fisher for a reorganised education system and 'professional' teachers influenced many of the elementary teachers. Resistance was not necessary with benevolent guardianship. At the same time as promises were made, an internal memo on 'teachers as civil servants' rejected this option – one of its reasons was that teachers would clearly recognise the nature of their employment and their employers!

The crisis in the relations between the state and its teachers was caused by the increased resistance of the teachers to their employers, their actions, their allies and ideas. It was also altered by the need for a reorganised education system for a capitalist state which needed to safeguard its survival and renew the accumulation of capital and the means of production halted by the war. The state was also consistent in its need to safeguard itself and the ruling class. The necessary accommodation with the teachers lasted only a few years. The Geddes 'cuts' and the resurgence of local authority attacks on the union or on individual teachers reduced the material gains of the 1918–20 settlement. 'Professionalism' as a gift of the state could now be seen partly as a controlling technique. Teachers were faced with a resurgence of strength among employers, without allies (as the unions were collapsing in membership) and divided amongst themselves, economically and politically.

The state appropriated part of the teacher's concern – a 'craft' concern for the quality of the product and the skills used in its creation, defined by teachers as the vital part of professionalism – and used part of it as a means of recognising and controlling them. The State reproduced the elements of the 'craft' concern which dealt with duty and service and excluded the part which dealt with autonomy, expertise and resistance. It created an ideology to license a group of workers and to cut them off from the recognition of their natural allies.

The difficulty that teachers, and white collar workers, as a whole, had in deciding where their interests lay was compounded by the powerful counter-attack waged by employers in the early Twenties. Economic cuts, the isolation and sacking of militants, attacks by local authorities and the emphasis on duty and service served the purpose of isolating teachers from the other members of the working class and demoralising them.

This period may reveal answers to questions of labour-power reproduction in schools. Why was the state threatened by teachers at this time? It had previously been content to control teachers indirectly but the awakening

of a strong class consciousness and alliance, in words and
deeds, with the Labour movement changed considerably
the way in which control operated and increased the
need for it to be effective. In the first decade, literature
was published which referred to the growing secular
power of teachers. How must this power have looked when
it could have combined with a socialist or a working class
curriculum? Is this too far fetched? W.G. Cove, later
reminiscing about this period, said that Fisher and Lloyd
George were very concerned at the restlessness of the
teachers and their bitterness – Lloyd George even referred
to the teachers involved in all the Continental revolu-
tionary movements of the time. The teacher was a social
danger to the state. The state proceeded to reinterpret
its public role to the teachers as being that of referee or
arbiter between them and their real employers, the local
authorities. The Burnham settlement was part of this
new role, and part of what Fisher had called 'harmonious'
relations between capital and labour. The creation of a
professional myth by the state was also a necessity –
harmony could exist when the state guaranteed the
teachers' living standard while dominating all discussion
of responsibilities and duties. The release of the elementary
school curriculum from state control was, perhaps, a part
of this new deal but an employee is always an employee.
The growth of the teacher Unions to defend conditions of
work and standards of living, against either the state (as
in the Geddes Committee proposals) or reactionary local
authorities, suggests that 'harmony' cannot be created by
sophistory alone. Incompatible interests defined the relationship. Like any other group of workers, resistance

Teachers, Professionalism and Class

moves between different levels, from the shopfloor and school to national campaigns, and it does so in different historical periods or in different locations. The tension between the teacher and the state may be expressed in many ways and in different strategies and tactics depending on the situation.

Professionalism, a concern for the quality of the service and the product and a defence of skilled labour when used by teachers, was not, for the teachers, limited to the state's concentration on duties and responsibilities. It all depends who defines responsibilities – employers or labour? At that time, as now, unionism and professionalism were not essentially divided – one was, and is, the expression of the other.

References

1 MORLEY, J. (1873) *The Struggle for National Education*, London, Champman Hall, p. 39.
2 NATIONAL UNION OF TEACHERS, (1909), Annual Report.
3 Quoted in WILLIAMS, R.A. (1953) 'The development of professional status among the elementary teachers under the school board 1870–1904', Unpublished Ph.D. thesis, London University.
4 *Ibid.*
5 *Ibid.*
6 *The Educational Times*, (1891) January, p. 29, quoted in PARRY, N. and PARRY, J. (1974) 'Teachers and professionalism: The failure of an occupational strategy', in FLUDE, M. and AHIER, J. *Educability, Schools and Ideology*, Croom Helm.
7 (1909) March, *Review of Incorporated Association of Headmasters*, quoted in BARON, G. (1953) 'The teachers registration movement', *British Journal of Educational Studies*, Vol. 2.
8 NATIONAL UNION OF TEACHERS, (1910), *Report of the Tenure Committee*.
9 NATIONAL UNION OF TEACHERS, (1913), *Report of the Tenure Committee*.
10 HAMILTON, H. (1917) *The Compleat Schoolmarm*.
11 *Birmingham Post*, (1913) 15 November.
12 NATIONAL UNION OF TEACHERS, (1917), *Annual Report*.
13 TROPP, A. (1957) *The School Teachers*, Heinemann, p. 208.
14 NATIONAL UNION OF TEACHERS, (1917), *Annual Report*.

Teachers and White Collar Unionism

15 Trades Union Congress, (1901), *34th Annual Report*, quoted in Simon; B. (1965) *Education and the Labour Movement 1870–1920*, Lawrence and Wishart.
16 *The Rhondda Socialist*, (1913) 15 March.
17 *The Schoolmaster*, (1917) 21 April.
18 *The Schoolmaster*, (1917) 10 November.
19 *The Schoolmaster*, (1917) 8 December.
20 *The Schoolmaster*, (1917) 10 November.
21 *The Daily Herald*, (1919) 21 April.
22 *The Times*, (1919) 17 April.
23 *The Times*, (1917) 1 March.
24 *The Times*, (1918) 12 December.
25 *Ibid.*
26 *The Socialist Review*, (1920) January–March, p. 59.
27 *The Times*, (1919) 26 January.
28 *The Rhondda Leader*, (1917) 20 October.
29 *The Rhondda Leader*, (1919) 29 March.
30 *The Times*, (1919) 1 May.
31 *The Daily Post*, (1877) 22 May, quoted in Anderson, G. (1976) *Victorian Clerks*, Manchester University Press. This discussion of the work of the clerk in the late nineteenth century is based on this work.
32 Spoor, A. (1967) *White Collar Union: Fifty Years of NALGO*, Heinemann.
33 *Ibid.*
34 *Ibid.*
35 *Ibid.*
36 *Ibid.*
37 Bain, G.S. (1968) *Growth of White Collar Unionism*, Oxford University Press.
38 Spoor, A. (1967) *op. cit.*
39 Many white collar unions were formed and recruited heavily in this period and several joined the TUC. See Bain, G.S. (1968) *op. cit.*
40 Most white collar unions were recognised by the employers during or immediately after the First World War. See Bain, G.S. (1968) *op. cit.*
41 Klingender, F.D. (1935) *The Condition of Clerical Labour in Britain*, London, Lawrence and Wishart.
42 The affiliation of CAWA, BISAKTA etc. See Bain, G.S. (1968) *op. cit.*
43 *The Clerk*, (1925) February, in Bain, G.S. (1968) *op. cit.*
44 Klingender, F.D. (1935) *op. cit.*
45 Spoor, A. (1967) *op. cit.*
46 Bain, G.S. (1968) *op. cit.*
47 Klingender, F.D. (1935) *op. cit.*
48 *Ibid.*
49 Walker, W.E. (1916) 'Are clerks workers?', *Plebs*, January, pp. 266–8.

Chapter 4.
Proletarianization

Proletarianization of the White Collar Worker

We have seen how teachers defended themselves against the attacks of the employer; how trades unionism was, and is, an important part in this defence. We have also seen that, whatever the difficulties those workers had in analysing and acting upon their class position and joining with other workers in act and ideology, they were always concerned about resisting the influence of the employer in the workplace. This resistance has been called 'professional autonomy' but we have distinguished between the 'craft' concern of professionalism and the attempt to control white collar workers by a diluted ideology of duty.

The process of resistance was, and is, necessary because of the changing and increasing demands of capital. Monopoly capital needs constantly to revolutionize the means of production in the process of concentrating and accumulating capital. In so doing, it alters the relations of production, the relations between the worker and the employer, the worker and work.

Proletarianization is the process whereby the worker is forced into a closer relationship with capital, which removes the skill (the conception and execution of work) and therefore the relative autonomy of the worker. The constant drive towards the accumulation of capital extends this process to more and more workers. The state is increasingly used in this process as a mediating agent. As Marx makes clear in the Communist Manifesto this process simplifies the nature of the class divisions in society:

> Society as a whole is more and more splitting up into two great hostile camps, into two great classes directly facing each other; Bourgeoisie and Proletariat.[1]

It is this argument that we wish to extend to teachers, firstly, by discussing the nature of white collar proletarianisation and secondly, by a tentative discussion of the way this process can be seen in education. In effect, we are trying to re-establish the major element of class analysis which has been ignored in recent discussions, and never applied thoroughly to teachers. We are also trying to continue a debate which was begun by, amongst others, W.G. Cove in the Rhondda Socialist.

Class is a relational concept, made up of ideological, social and economic features. Here, we are trying to establish through an examination of the economic process of proletarianization, the consequences for teachers' assessment of their class position, which are not merely economic, but are reflected in connected political and ideological developments. Having established the outline, we wish to analyse its effect on white collar work.

The Victorian clerk working in a small office, with general duties, educated and in a close relationship with an employer whose family he might marry into, is far removed from the clerk in industry today; the work is specialized, routinized, graded and concentrated. The boundaries that clearly divided the clerk from the labourer have diminished – manual labour is now part of office work, machines dominate office work and control it, supervisors are increasing in number. Capital, especially monopoly capital, altered and changed the work and in so doing, as we have noted, altered the relations of production. New skills demanded by a changing capital, using new techniques made radical changes in job structures. There was an increasing demand for clerks, administrators and other personnel.

J.R. Dale discussing the technical change which altered offices, talks of increased mechanisation, specialisation and size:

The specialised organisation of work preceded the

commercial use of the typewriter and the calcula-
tor, but these reacted, in turn, upon the work to
bring about radical alterations in systems and
methods. The punched card installation in the
first quarter of the present century, and the elec-
tronic computer in the 1950s, are merely important
items in a long series of innovation.[2]

Since that was written, micro-computers and word
processors are, in turn, altering clerical work. The
physical organisation of the clerk's workplace has altered
in consequence of the mechanisation:

As the machines increase in number and complexity, they give rise to further divisions of labour
to add to those which, originally, they were called
to implement. Their costs rise, and as installations
become larger, there is a strong tendency to
centralisation; the physical aspect of the office
becomes more like that of the factory department,
and the nature of the routines changes from the
purely clerical to the manual or technical. . . . The
impact of technical change is altering both the
kind of work which has to be done and the conditions in which it is done.[3]

Most of the clerical work now takes place in large,
open rooms – partitions, panels, larger desks or private
offices are reserved for the various kinds of supervisors
and managers. Most of the work needs to be done in
specialized areas, (Export, Accounts, Stock Control etc.),

either manually or by mechanical means requiring little, if any, discretion or skill and increasingly threatened by new technological innovation. A worker in one of these areas has little chance to understand the process of the whole enterprise. The Apprenticeship system has ended. The gap between the clerk and the supervisor will grow with mechanization:

> Future commercial executives will require a much higher standard of general education; a thorough understanding of the economic system; a knowledge of the fundamental principles of accounting ... Moreover a good general knowledge of scientific method and industrial processes will be needed as well as high qualities of leadership.[4]

Mechanization then alters the work and the relationships of work. Supervisors grow in number and so do machine controllers. It is increasingly hard to be promoted out of the specialization.

If clerical work was like a 'craft' then the technological changes and the consequent new work organisation have broken down or eliminated it. Consequently, like other craft workers, the clerks have lost control over the basis of their power, even if it was rarely used because of the stronger paternal relationship within which they worked. The traditions, rules and codes of conduct of the office based on 'craft' have been broken down. As Braverman notes, although the clerical worker had few tools to speak of, being a clerk meant being involved in:

> a total occupation, the object of which was to keep

current the records of the financial and operating condition of the enterprise, as well as its relations with the external world. Master craftsmen such as book-keepers or chief clerks, maintained control over the process in its totality and apprentices or journeymen craftsmen – ordinary clerks, copying clerks, office boys – learned their crafts in office apprenticeships and in the ordinary course of events advanced through the levels by promotion.[5]

The 'total' occupation is gone and, with it, the prospect of promotion through the occupation and identification with it. Control over the work is now closely supervised.

the intimate associations, the atmosphere of mutual obligation, and the degree of loyalty which characterised the small office became transformed . . . the characteristic feature of this era was the ending of the reign of the book-keeper and the rise of the office manager as the prime functionary and representative of higher management.[6]

Apart from office managers, supervisory staff have been growing in proportion to the workforce. Even mechanization has not eroded the number of supervisors – mechanization has eliminated the skilled and semi-skilled but they have often been re-skilled as supervisors. In white collar work, this may mean a supervisory role plus the ordinary work role. Aronovitz has discussed the lack of productivity of these workers, even with mechanisation:

Much of this growth [of office workers] is due to

the expansion of supervisory position at a more
rapid rate than the clerical workers working under
them in these last two decades. Often managerial
status disguises work that was formerly part of the
duties of the non-supervisory stratum. ... The
effort to boost productivity by proliferating supervisory personnel is a tacit recognition that resistance to work routines among office and sales
workers is as widespread as among the more
militant groups of manual workers.[7]

Supervisory staff generate a great deal of correspondence
as the work increases in complexity or is sub-divided.
There is little or no autonomy in the work of either the
supervisor or the worker – the tasks and the descriptions
are set and standardised.

A feature of clerical work noted by observers is that
comprehension of the whole process and control over it is
now lost. As far as it is possible to labour without thought,
then this is the life of the office for many. It is manual
labour for most of them, repetition and routine. As
technological innovation develops, thinking will be restricted to a re-skilled minority. As Braverman suggests,
for many:

The work is still performed in the brain but the
brain is used as the equivalent of the hand of the
detail worker in production, grasping and re-
leasing a single piece of 'data' over and over again.[8]

Now clerical production techniques will, as they will on

the shopfloor, increase control over the clerical worker by management. Control will be built into the tasks demanded by the machine – the order, speed and number will all be defined, out of the worker's control.

Aronovitz believes that a contradiction is present, in this process of standardisation and mechanisation between:

> the expectations generated by their training and the boredom and rate of their work tasks, between the degree of responsibility they possess for the production process and the absence of power to control more than its quantitative, and within set limits, qualitative adjustment.[9]

Aronovitz is talking here of the new generation of the de-skilled; the technical clerical staff and front-line supervisors who, at one time, could have expected to be promoted to middle management. He argues that management is unlikely to be recruited from technical staff of this quality because 'management' itself is now an occupation with its own training and concerns, particularly that of a 'control' function.

Apprenticeship is no longer necessary; 'craft' itself has gone; the general clerk vanished. For the mass of workers, jobs are interchangeable; there are no traditions, practices or autonomous divisions to be made. Simple tasks characterize the office, like the factory. Caplow, quoted in Braverman, makes it clear that

> a minimum command of the number system, the written language[10]

and a mechanical dexterity are required for these jobs, making each worker, clerical or industrial, the same – standard products of the education process. The same argument, of proletarianization, holds true for public service agencies – white collar workers in national or local departments concerned with health, social security employment and so on.

A difficulty already noted in discussing the class location of many white collar workers is the degree to which they create surplus value by selling their labour power. Indeed, some deny that these workers are exploited at all! Yet capital seeks profit everywhere and in everything – from toys to social policies. Many jobs produce profit in ways which are not immediately realizable – the product is rarely brought directly to the market place. Yet capital only employs workers because they increase the productivity of capital – not for philanthropic or charitable reasons. Indeed, (as much as possible) capital has consistently shown that at the first opportunity it tries to shed labour, temporarily or permanently. Capital's investment in machines and new technology has, as its main purpose, the increase of capital and the reduction of the number of wage earners. All workers employed by Capital are exploited – unpaid for labour time is always extracted. White collar workers, as far as it is possible to differentiate them today, are necessary to allocate, measure, transfer, improve or help to realise surplus value.

To summarize, the process of proletarianization is the result of the expansion of capitalist production and the concentration and centralisation of capital. This process de-personalizes employer/worker relations, breaks down

131

'craft' skills, increases technological investment (fixed to variable capital ratio), automates and de-skills, separates conception from the execution of work and increases management control over workers, their skills and the pace of their work. It continues the division of society into employers and workers, eliminating contradictory class locations in so doing.

Proletarianization and Teachers

In what ways can the process of proletarianization, described so far in relation to clerks, administrative and technical workers, be applied to teachers? Has the education service industry de-skilled its workforce through a constant technological change? Has the teacher lost craft skills and control over work (control over the conception as well as execution functions of work)? Has the teacher been seen as a unit in process of production, with the mass of teachers operating routinized, standardized tasks, and the remainder acting as supervisors and managers?

Questions such as these seem, strangely enough, to be absent from studies of teaching. Proletarianization would not easily fit the common notion of improvement or progress in education, nor can it easily be absorbed into new neo-Marxist schools of ideological or cultural determination in which teachers play a privileged, important role under capitalism.

Yet the education system has been tied ever more closely to the demands of the industrial needs of capitalism. These demands are for economy and efficiency and for the necessary education of the new workforce. Education has taken over the old 'apprenticeship to craft' schemes and produces a product roughly geared to the demands of capital though, at different times, these may be at variance with each other; a quiet, disciplined workforce or a flexible, highly educated workforce are perhaps not so much incompatible demands but come from different parts of industry at different levels of production. In an interesting pamphlet on just this issue, some teachers see the aim of the system as two-fold.

> first to make schools and colleges more productive in the sense of getting more people through exams with less expenditure on salaries and materials; and secondly, to ensure that what is taught is more relevant to a de-skilled and proletarianised economic structure. . . . [11]

The training for obedience, which has been consistently noted from the late Nineteenth Century to today, in the education of the working class product has been paralleled by an education for leadership or management for the middle classes. The product has been overtly described as being graded by 'ability' and 'intelligence', and this replaced the cruder forms of social control operated in the Revised Code. In the 1890s changes in the Regulations governing teachers were made that allowed the classification of children by ability and not by age. By the early 1920s, the creation of a specialized educational grading process, intelligence testing, legitimated the division of two educational products. This function has been revived at different periods as a more direct and useful (to the employing class) means of controlling the content and output of the educational product than the examination system, which has only operated in increasing frequency since the 2nd World War. Both methods are used to grade and sort the educational product but, in periods when it is unclear what product is demanded or when the means of actual control of the output has been weakened or when new demands of Capital supersede earlier demands, intelligence testing seems to act as a clearly defined management intervention tool, as opposed to examinations which keep the system running. Similar, perhaps, to the alteration, by work study methods (time and motion/Taylorism), of the pace of the production line jobs – certainly it defines the course of the teacher's work by external procedures not controlled by them.

The structure of the education system has altered as the demands of capital changed. The definition of efficiency and productivity altered. Industrial and commercial rivalry and innovations needed a specialized technical and supervisory staff; at different periods, these were produced in turn by the Central or Higher Grade schools, the Secondary Technical schools, the Grammar Schools, the 6th Forms, and then the Universities. As specialization increased and yet the numbers, in proportion, dropped, the centres producing these workers declined in number and relative position in the system. Re-structuring of the workforce and the educational requirements needed are constants.

As the technical demands of the employing class on the bulk of the educational product grew less, the social demands seem to have increased. Most schools seem to

Proletarianization

represent a declining concern for skilling and grading
pupils through examinations and an increasing concern
for the disciplining and ideological control functions of
schooling; an emphasis away from the curriculum departments towards the pastoral network. It is a paradox that
the rise of the examination industry now serves the purpose
of screening for unemployment or routinized white collar
or factory jobs. Examinations were once used to select
or grade the product for further stages of labour power
development yet, because of the devaluation of skill, they
now serve mainly as the maximum development of labour
power needed for most work today.[12] The de-skilling of
work and unemployment needs a minimum of 'real'
education – today, defined as English, Maths and possibly
Science; sometimes with the addition of Crafts or Art,
for its ability to encourage manipulative skills (needed in
office or factory work). School subjects are being proletarianized or de-skilled; for most pupils 'integrated'
subjects appeared as the replacement for 'subjects' (access
to 'subjects' being restricted to certain pupils selected as
technical or supervisory prospects) others were excluded
from certain skills. These new subjects, while ostensibly
based on 'relevance', appear in reality as low-grade
material in which value has been replaced by social
control. The content and pedagogy used reduces the
'craft' of the teachers and their consequent control over
the subject.

Schools have been increasingly brought within the
State's direct change, particularly as a servicing agency
for industry and also for social control. As the social
administration of 'welfare' capitalism with its strong

135

element of social control grew, so the kind of work done in the school altered. Teacher's duties increased and specialized parts of the school grew to connect directly with these social agencies. Duties such as liaising with medical and social welfare workers over the new health provisions of the late nineteenth century, or school attendance officers, or supervising milk distribution or school meal provision grew throughout the twentieth century. Teachers administrated the National Savings Scheme and collected money in the classroom.[13] In wartime, schools acted as one of the key agencies of social administration: in evacuation duties; the increased provision of food and milk; and even responsibility for factory workers children before and after school. A memo of the Board of Education[14] said:

> [The duties] have reached a volume which seriously interferes with the teacher's primary duty of teaching.

Hilsum and Cave (in 1971) described the clerical and mechanical tasks which make up twenty per cent of the teacher's day included marking attendance and dinner registers (80 per cent), filling records (of visits etc.), forms or lists (medical inspection etc.) and recording marks and checking library cards.[15]

The pastoral departments of secondary schools seem to have been created in response to this increased emphasis on the disciplinary or control function of mass schooling. It is closely connected to other state agencies, such as the police, school psychological service, Education Welfare

Department and the Probation Service. This work is now specialized and tends to be excluded from the daily work of the class teacher, even in its counselling aspect – a kind of 'production' control, in fact, eliminating 'line' difficulties. Withdrawal centres for 'disturbed' children continue this development.

As schools have grown, promotion for the teacher has altered. At the turn of the century, it was becoming difficult for certificated teachers to become Headteachers, due to the increased number of teachers and schools which were growing in size. The division between the class teacher and the Headteacher widened; separate associations grew within the NUT. The national salary scales demanded by the Union were altered by the Burnham Committee into four scales, based on geographical location – cities, towns, rural districts etc. The Urban Scale was the most remunerative. At the same time, a marginal pool of money was allowed for discretionary above-scale payments to teachers for additional managerial responsibilities. This increased after the second World War. Grades and scales have grown rapidly in the post-war period; graded posts were created in 1956, a career structure in 1970, a senior teacher scale in 1973. The differentials between the different scales (particularly, between the class teacher and top management) increased and scale posts were given (discretionarily by management) for increased productivity ('extra responsibility'). Teachers had to attend managerial re-skilling courses and their new jobs decreased teaching time; a supervisory and managerial staff had been created amongst teachers. Deputy headteachers had jobs increasingly defined in 'production' terms; timetables needed complex mathematical and managerial skills in the larger comprehensive schools, as did the curriculum – new posts of curriculum co-ordinators (middle managers) often involved new management powers in the school (attending all department meetings, surveying the work of the school as a whole, supervising new arrangements).

Educational administration became an area of study in its own right, separated from, but influenced by, industrial management theory. Schools are analysed in terms of crucial productivity factors such as their management style (collegial etc.), their organisational 'climate', the role of the headteacher and even their creativity (adopting or adapting change). Schools are affected by large scale management exercises using systems analysis and job description, or industrial Research and Development efficiency or de-skilling exercises.

As productivity is increased, the capital invested in schools is constantly checked or reduced; school capitation allowances decline, school book buying decreases, new building provision is reduced.[16] Most of all, teacher's pay (in common with other workers) has been reduced in a series of national pay freezes, class size has not decreased and, in some areas, is increasing due to the 'cuts'. The state is even beginning to distinguish between its needs and those of parents by encouraging the latter to fund the activities and resources of the school.

Indeed, a major consequence of the cuts has been to make teachers aware of their similarities with other wage earners. As spending on education declines, along with the school population, then the idea of teaching as a career is eroded as promotion prospects recede, guaranteed employment becomes a thing of the past and job security disappears. All these characteristics of teaching, which marked it off from conventional wage labour in the 1960s, have been eroded in the 1980s. As a consequence, teachers are turning to employment legislation – which codifies employee's rights and employer's duties – as a defensive strategy. No longer able to assume shared professional commitment to the preservation of the education service between teachers and their technical employers, the local agents of the state particularly in 'corporate' authorities, where educational provision has suffered in the reallocation of priorities from the centre towards the maintenance of law and order and defence spending.

Thus even teachers who totally reject any parallels between their situation and that of the British steel workers are having to appeal to a common core of protective legislation when faced with redeployment, and are learning the extent of their vulnerability when they no longer fulfill a function useful to capital. There has been a considerable increase in union activity in relation to redeployment and redundancy. Teachers, faced with such issues in increasing numbers, and conscious of the reserve pool of trained, unemployed teachers, see their only possible strategy in union organisation and resistance.

An allied development has been the growth of codification of teachers' terms and conditions of service, so long confused by local 'agreements' about the 'professionalism' or otherwise of supervizing children waiting for school transport, playing in playgrounds, eating school dinners and so on. These duties were very often fulfilled by teachers in the past because of their reluctance to put unsupervized children at risk, a danger greatly emphasised by the employing authorities who were quick to underline the disastrous consequences of such neglect of professional duty. Teachers thus fulfilled unpaid, non-contractual 'voluntary' duties which diluted their claim to professional expertise and saved the employers considerable sums through the non-employment of auxiliary and ancillary staff. Though there had been an element of organised teacher resistance to these duties (the success fight against the compulsion to supervise school meals), resistance only grew in strength when teachers, like other workers, became caught in the wages freeze, which caused an extensive re-examination of their hours of unpaid labour. Despite employer resistance, the pressure from organised teachers for a contract which specifies their contractual obligations has grown. Nor have organised teachers conceded to employer demands that this question be considered as part of salary negotiations.

Thus these factors, given considerable force by the economic situation, the declining school population, and the State's willingness to scapegoat teachers as part of its drive to rationalize education, have continued to force teachers into a re-examination of the real strengths and weaknesses of their relationships with their employer. In so doing, they have embraced the strategies and adapted the experience of other workers who have more widespread experience of resistance or a stronger collective sense of their past.

Even that area of teacher's work that seemed most

140

closely related to their claims to professional autonomy, the curriculum, reveals tendencies towards proletarianization. Since the state de-regulated elementary school regulations in 1926 with regard to the curriculum, it has been argued that teachers, in partnership with local authorities and the DES, control the curriculum. This situation, it is also argued, is threatened today by the Assessment of Performance Unit (a national monitoring unit on assessment), the reorganisation of the Schools Council, The Green Paper, and so on. Our argument would suggest that teachers never had curricular autonomy, except in the sense of deciding when to operate the machine and what was a reasonable output. The production line, its pace, content and product have been broadly defined for teachers and altered as the demands of capital altered. It de-skilled teachers by routinizing their work, excluding 'craft' control and involving increased, specialized supervision.

If our curriculum was autonomously decided by teachers it would not, in the secondary sector, show the degree of congruence between schools that it does; not only the subjects but their time allotment is the same from school to school. External supervision and control, in the form of examinations, the Inspectorate, training norms etc., influenced and shaped the curriculum. As school management became more closely aligned with external management, the headteachers and senior staff act increasingly as the quality/quantity control. Controls have been built into the system, in its organisational structure, in its management and state professional ideologies, in its apoliticization, which control teachers.

Control may be in different forms; teachers may acquiesce or agree with demands made upon them, they have a concern for 'public service', they may work to survive. In other words, whether teachers agree or not with what they are asked to do is irrelevant. All workers work to survive. Without work they cease to be able to continue. Many workers disagree with the processes and ideas they are asked to operate. They have no choice but to fulfill them though they also resist them – by controlling the pace of the work, by disputing management's right to manage, by striking. Much of the curriculum innovation literature discusses the resistance by teachers to outside productivity innovations – regardless of the content of the innovation, its form is seen as determining. Curriculum innovation is a deliberate and faster form of a process which has been going for a long time – the de-skilling of teachers.

Michael Apple, in a discussion of curriculum change in a perspective of proletarianization concludes:

> When jobs are de-skilled, the knowledge that once accompanied it, knowledge that was controlled and used by workers in carrying out their day to day lives on their jobs, goes somewhere. Management attempts (with varying degrees of success) to accumulate and control this assemblage of skills and knowledge. It attempts, in other words, to separate conception from execution. The control of knowledge enables management to plan; the worker should ideally merely carry these plans out to the specifications, and at the pace, set by people

away from the actual point of production.[17]

This form of control is present in the pre-packaged sets of curricular materials found in private enterprise catalogues or in nationalized industry catalogues (teacher's centres, Schools Councils, Resource Centres). All aspects of the curriculum are defined – its purpose, content, pedagogy etc. Apple continues:

> Skills that teachers used to need, that were deemed essential to the craft of working with children – such as curriculum deliberation and planning, designing teaching and curricular strategies for specific groups and individuals based on intimate knowledge of these people – are no longer necessary.[18]

Apple also argues that for some teachers, re-skilling of the teachers with management ideologies and control strategies are substituted for 'craft' skills.

Thus we would argue that the concept of proletarianization does have value as an explanatory device when applied to an analysis of teachers' class location. Through this process teachers are not merely made more like other workers in economic terms, i.e. less economically advantaged, more vulnerable to redundancy and pressure towards increased workload. The proletarianization process also involves a loss of control over the work process, a loss of definition by the worker of the essential elements of the task. Thus the teachers broad self-image as an 'educator' is eroded and his/her function as a processor

stressed. This in turn breaks down the teachers' individ-
ualistic professional self image, and forces on them a
revived recognition of a collective interest in organization
against the employer.

References

1 MARX, K. and ENGELS, F. (1848) *The Communist Manifesto*, Moscow, Progress
Publications, (1966), p. 40.
2 DALE, J.R. (1962) *The Clerk in Industry*, Liverpool University Press, p. 81.
3 *Ibid.*
4 Quoted in DALE, J.R. (1962) *op. cit.* Management Abstracts, (1958) March.
5 BRAVERMAN, H. (1974) *Labor and Monopoly Capital*, New York, Monthly Review
Press.
6 *Ibid.*
7 ARONOVITZ, S. (1974) *False Promises: The Shaping of American Working Class Consciousness*, New York, McGraw Hill, p. 301.
8 BRAVERMAN, H. (1974) *op. cit.*, p. 319.
9 ARONOVITZ, S. (1974) *op. cit.*, p. 306.
10 CAPLOW, T. (1954) *Sociology of Work*, Minnesota, quoted in BRAVERMAN, H.
(1974) *op. cit.*
11 'The crisis in education', *Big Flame*, (1977), April.
12 The proportion of children, between 1971–75, leaving schools with qualifications
rose from 55 per cent to 88 per cent. *The Guardian*, (1976) 11 August, (quoted in
Big Flame).
13 In the time of dispute, in the 1950s, teachers withdrew from this service as they
did from compulsory school meals supervision.
14 Board of Education (1941) Memorandum. Quoted in GOSDEN, P. (1972) *The
Evolution of a Profession*, Basil Blackwell.
15 HILSUM, S. and CAVE, B.S. (1971) *The Teacher's Day*, National Foundation for
Educational Research.
16 For example, London has reduced, in new buildings, classroom space from 41
square feet, in 1966–67, to $38\frac{1}{2}$ square feet, in 1969, to 33 square feet in 1973.
Times Educational Supplement, (1973) 25 May.
17 APPLE, M. (1981) 'Curriculum form and the logic of technical control', in BARTON,
L., MEIGHAN, R. and WALKER, S. (Eds.) *Schooling, Ideology and the Curriculum*,
Barcombe, The Falmer Press, p. 000.
18 *Ibid.*

Some Tentative Conclusions

Throughout the book we have moved towards taking up a particular position on the class location of organised teachers. In the first section of the book, we criticized the use of the concept of professionalism to assign teachers to a middle class social class location, to characterize them as collaborators with the state, and to mark them off from other workers who were unionized. We suggested that the concept of professionalism had not been fully developed in terms of its strategic importance to monopoly capitalism as an ideology which denied class conflict and co-opted key groups of workers into the bureaucratised state. We also argued that professionalism, as an ideology, presents management problems, in that it reinforces a craft ethic in these workers which sets up pressures for autonomy in the professional task and concern for the service offered. All these contradictory and ambivalent strands within professionalism need to be understood and developed, rather than presenting simple dichotomies between it as a descriptive concept on the one hand and unionism on the other.

We also criticised Marxist and neo-Marxist approaches to teachers' class location, which drew on assumptions about the meaning of professionalism to teachers which condemned them for invoking it to separate themselves ideologically from the working class. We contended that teachers are workers exploited, like other workers, by capital and not isolated from them in a new middle class. We suggested that the creation of a 'new middle class' as a location for problematic white collar workers is a theoretical solution which depends on an acceptance of antagonistic class relations between these workers and the rest of the labour force which cannot be convincingly demonstrated. Indeed the basis for this antagonism seems to us to depend on the unwarranted assumption that these workers collaborate with the state at the ideological and political levels.

The limited exploration of professionalism as a concept, in conjunction with a theoretical demarcation of teachers from other workers, has led to emphasis on their ambivalence and contradictory class location, all combining to separate organised teacher behaviour from the behaviour of other organised workers. Yet, as we have attempted to demonstrate, this analysis depends on a very partial view of teacher union history (itself very closely linked to a limited conception of professionalism) and a perspective which ignores changes and developments in the objective conditions of work for all white collar employees, including teachers.

To sum up, our position is that teachers are workers, who have used professionalism strategically and had it used against them, that they have allied with organised labour in the past and, as a consequence of pressures for proletarianization, may develop such alliances and strategies again.

Yet, as we said at the outset, this book does not claim to offer proof of our position. Our intention was to reveal some of the assumptions behind the conventional characterization of teachers (a convention given strength by authors of both the Left and the Right), to question these assumptions and suggest at least two alternative ways of looking at teachers – through a reinterpreted history and in conjunction with white collar workers. Finally we wanted to give to proletarianization a greater weight than it has in the neo-Marxist literature, where it has mainly been restricted to the economic sphere or to comparisons being drawn between the school and the factory. We feel that the process of proletarianization attacks the teachers idea of professionalism at its roots – the 'service' idea and the notion of autonomy. If these are destroyed, then the use of professionalism as a controlling ideology by the state is weakened, and the supposed conflict between professionalism and unionism is more clearly seen as the use of union strategies to defend the last traces of a 'craft' ideal.

Teachers, Professionalism and Class

We recognise the speculative nature of this discussion, and do not wish to condemn others for categorizing workers at an abstract, theoretical level without adequate evidence while committing that crime ourselves. Again we must stress that this book is an attempt to generate debate, to suggest alternative perspectives which might lead to more empirical work in a rather neglected area. Grace, in his *Teachers, Ideology and Control*, suggested that there was agreement among sociologists of differing theoretical perspectives about the need to locate teachers structurally within the social formation. That attempt has, to date, resulted in the structural location of teachers in ambiguity. We wish to locate teachers positively in their class. We think that to do so requires much more detailed investigation of teachers' work and teachers' actions – exploring their contradictions and placing them at the centre of a dynamic process. We hope that, by raising the issues in this book, we can at least resurrect that possibility.

Index

control of 8, 14, 27, 30, 34, 98, 135, 141
elementary 71
expenditure 46, 138
improvement 24, 25, 83, 91
social selection mechanism 19
secondary 71
state 3
educational administration 138
educational policy 22–24, 27, 88
educational standards 21, 26, 28, 33, 74, 84, 85
Ehrenreich, B. and Ehrenreich, J. 45, 48, 53
Engels, F. (see Marx and Engels)
Equal Pay League 73
equality 28
of opportunity 52
examinations 98, 133–135, 141
Education Department 75, 77

falling rolls 140
Finn, D., Grant, N. and Johnson, R. 56, 57
Fisher, 90, 91, 92, 109, 117, 119
Flexner, A. 12
Flude, M. and Ahier, J. 120

Ginsberg, M., Mayenn, R. and Miller, H. 44, 49
Gintis, H. (see Bowles and Gintis)
Gosden, P.H.J.H. 2, 5, 6
Gould, Sir R. 28
Grant, N. (see Finn et al)

Hamilton, H. 80, 120
hegemony 52
Hilsum, S. and Cave, B.S. 136, 144
Her Majesty's Inspectorate (HMI's) 74, 141
Howard, W. 93
Hunt, A. 46, 49, 50, 60

ideology 10, 14–17, 19–20, 35, 40, 51–53, 55, 60, 62, 67, 92, 113, 118, 123–124, 141, 143, 145–147
intelligence testing 98, 133
interest groups (see pressure groups)

Jarvis, F. 25
Johnson, R. (see Finn et al)
Johnson, T.J. 11, 17, 19, 20, 21, 22, 30, 35, 47

Kekewich, Sir G. 7, 71
Klingender, F.D. 110, 111, 121
knowledge, development of 21
Kogan, M. 23, 25, 26, 27, 28, 30, 32

labour
apathy of 110
autonomy of 40, 123–124, 129, 148
as commodity 40–41, 44–45, 96, 104, 112, 131
control of 44, 101, 104, 124, 127, 128, 130, 132, 142, 143
de-skilling 100–101, 118, 130, 132, 135
differentiation of 102, 107–108, 111–113, 133–134
division of 42, 46–48, 53
exploitation of 41–42, 44, 47, 49, 51, 58, 60, 88, 95, 112, 116, 131, 148
and industrial action 111, 142
mental and manual 50–51, 53, 59, 100–101, 103, 111–112, 116, 125, 129, 131
militancy of 61, 103, 105, 129
organized 10, 31, 56
and party politics 103, 106–108
productive/unproductive 47, 49, 58, 59

Index

reproduction of 44, 52, 62
re-skilling 128–129
shortage of 106
socialization of 52, 56, 62, 133, 135
solidarity of 90, 102, 113–114
white collar 48, 60–61, 68, 98–101, 103–109, 111–114, 124–130, 135, 146–147
Larson, M.S. 11, 18, 30
Lloyd George, D. 119
local education authorities 9, 26, 28–30, 32, 68, 70–71, 73, 79, 81–84, 92, 97, 99, 104, 106, 108–109, 114, 116, 118–119, 139, 141
Locke, M. 26, 28, 29

MacDonald, R. 91
Maclean, J. 86
Manning, L. 86
Marx, K. 40, 41, 45, 46, 47, 48, 53, 59, 60
Marx, K. and Engels, F. 144
Marxist theory 42–43, 45, 56, 58, 94, 132–133, 146–147
Maxton, J. 86
Mayenn, R. (see Ginsberg et al)
Meighan, R. (see Barton et al)
Miller, H. (see Ginsberg et al)
Millerson, G. 11
Miners Federation (MFGB) 111
Morley, J. 120
Morant, R. 78
Morris, M. 25, 28

National Association of Local Government Officers 101–106, 108, 110, 111
National Association of School-masters (NAS) 28, 29
National Federation of Class Teachers 73

National Federation of Women Teachers 73
National Poor Law Officers Association 102
National Union of Clerks (see also Clerk's Union) 102
National Union of Teachers (NUT) 3–6, 8–10, 15, 28–29, 31–32, 34–35, 68–72, 76–86, 89–90, 92–97, 102–109, 137

Olin Wright, E. 55

parents 138
Parry, N. and Parry, J. 14, 15, 16, 18, 20
payment by results 8
Plebs League 94, 111
Poulantzas, N. 48, 52, 53, 54, 55, 59
power 17, 23, 26, 33, 52, 119
pressure groups 1, 10, 12, 21–33
productivity 129, 131, 137, 138, 142
professionalism 2, 10–13, 16–18, 20–22, 33–34, 39–40, 57–58, 62, 67, 87–88, 91–92, 99, 101, 103, 109, 115–120, 124, 139, 145–147
process approach to 13
professionalization 8, 18, 34
professions 1, 12, 16, 42, 54
class analysis of 17
legal and medical 12–13
skills 40
sociology of 1–2, 11, 12, 17
state 17–20, 30
proletarianization 60–61, 68, 74, 124–125, 131–133, 135, 141–143

Ray, G. 94
Revised Code 74, 77, 133

151

Index